Foundations of the Mind

Foundations of the Mind

Children's Understanding of Reality

Eugene V. Subbotsky

With a Foreword by James V. Wertsch

Harvard University Press
Cambridge, Massachusetts
1993

Copyright © 1992 by Eugene V. Subbotsky
All rights reserved
Printed in the United States of America
10 9 8 7 6 5 4 3 2 1

This book is printed on acid-free paper, and its binding
materials have been chosen for strength and durability.

Library of Congress Cataloging-in-Publication Data
Subbotsky, Eugene V.
  Foundations of the mind : children's understanding of reality /
  Eugene V. Subbotsky ; with a foreword by James V. Wertsch.
    p. cm.
  Includes bibliographical references and indexes.
  ISBN 0-674-31187-6 (alk. paper)
  1. Perception in children. 2. Reality in children. 3. Piaget,
Jean, 1896– . I. Title.
BF723.P36S833 1992   92-43746
155.4'13—dc20   CIP

Contents

Foreword

James V. Wertsch

In 1984, while in Moscow as a Fulbright Lecturer, I had the opportunity to meet Eugene Subbotsky. During previous visits to the USSR I had frequently heard his colleagues refer to him as one of the brightest and most productive psychologists of his generation in that country, so it was with great interest that I went to see him. We met on a raw, gray November day at the Psychology Faculty of Moscow State University and discussed common interests and acquaintances for about an hour. Then he told me about his research and asked if I would like to participate in some of his experimental tasks. The tasks he used, which are described in the present volume, involved a box in which stamps and other objects seem to appear, disappear, and undergo transformations.

Subbotsky began by showing me a small, felt-lined wooden box. He asked me to examine it thoroughly and then gave me an ordinary postage stamp to place in it. When I had done so, he asked me to move the stamp slightly so that it was centered on the bottom of the box, something that perhaps would have tipped me off to what followed had I been more sophisticated about the techniques used by magicians. Then, after closing the box, he asked me to watch closely as he passed his hands over it several times and tugged on what appeared to be invisible cords extending from the two sides. I watched all this, I must confess, with a somewhat bemused attitude.

He then asked me to open the box. The stamp I had placed in it was not there, and I had no hint as to why. On subsequent trials I witnessed what appeared to be other transformations of stamps. For example, after

vii

he had carried out the mysterious actions with his hands, a frayed version of what had been a new stamp or torn up pieces of the original stamp appeared when I opened the box.

As I remember it now, my reaction over the course of these trials changed from one of bemusement to one of agnosticism. I was at a loss to produce a normal, scientifically grounded explanation of what was going on, and I had not formed an alternative account based on hypnosis, psychic forces, or anything else. I should note for those readers whose main acquaintance with Soviet psychology might have come from popular Western books of the 1960s and 1970s about "psychic discoveries behind the Iron Curtain" that at no time did I think I was engaged in an experiment in parapsychology. Instead, I simply had no explanation for what I was seeing and became increasingly ready to admit as much.

Then Subbotsky began to ask me a series of questions about possible explanations. Among other things he asked me whether I could rule out the possibility that he had exerted some kind of psychic power to alter the contents of the box or that some magic force was involved. I felt a bit uneasy, if not ridiculous, in admitting to such possibilities, but I had, after all, inspected the box and been unable to find anything about it that would produce a normal, scientifically acceptable explanation, one grounded in what Subbotsky terms "everyday realities." Furthermore, I do not remember contemplating breaking off my participation in the session, something that might readily have been predicted on the basis of Dembo's (1967) classic studies showing that subjects tend to remain in an experimental "space" even under trying circumstances.

What did happen was that I felt the solid ground of normal, scientific rationality begin to slip away, and I found myself starting to entertain ideas about psychic forces and so forth—alternatives I would usually be loathe to consider in professional discussions with colleagues. Overall, the most striking aspect of the whole experience was that this transition in my beliefs and thinking had occurred so easily and so quickly.

Since my participation in Subbotsky's experiment, I have often thought about the lesson it taught me. In particular, I think of it when I read, review, or produce studies documenting the development of rational processes in children or the uses of rationality among adults. Countless studies of this sort and, more generally, major segments of the discipline of psychology are based on implicit and largely unexamined assumptions about the ready acceptance and ubiquity of rationality in everyday realities. Subbotsky's studies suggest that we have thought all too little about how we deal with what he calls "unusual realities." Of course, some areas of psychology are specifically devoted to nonrational mental processes, and this has been widely accepted as appropriate at least since Freud's time. However, his studies suggest that even when we think our focus is rational cognition, we should reexamine some basic assumptions.

In areas such as the psychology of cognition and cognitive development one of these assumptions is that once a form of rational cognition emerges it would be nonsensical and quite unusual to slip back, or regress, to previous, nonrational forms of thinking. It is precisely this assumption that I came to question more and more as a result of the experience of finding myself giving up the rationality of everyday reality so readily after a few minutes of participating in Subbotsky's study.

Subbotsky has managed to develop his insights into these issues by drawing on, but going far beyond, existing theoretical frameworks. His formulation is influenced heavily by Piaget, and as is to be expected of a psychologist who spent much of the 1960s and 1970s at Moscow State University, he also draws on Vygotsky and his followers. However, his ideas can hardly be reduced to those of either of these figures, given their assumptions about the power and ubiquity of rationality. These assumptions are widely recognized in the case of Piaget, who is often characterized as viewing children's development in terms of their action as "little scientists." It is perhaps less widely recognized in the case of Vygotsky, since he drew on ideas from drama, literary theory, and so forth when formulating his approach. However, as a member of a generation sincerely dedicated to building a new society on the basis of scientific principles, Vygotsky was committed to rationality in a way that would seem quite surprising to many of us today.

Figures such as Piaget and Vygotsky would have some difficulty dealing with indications that someone who demonstrates scientific rationality in one setting would want to do anything "lower" in another. They viewed scientific rationality as a "telos" (Kaplan, 1967) of development, and it is hard to view deviations from this telos, once it is reached, as anything other than a kind of theoretically embarrassing regression (Tulviste, 1991). Much of the ingenuity of Subbotsky's studies is that they show that it is not all that unusual to find such deviations in adults, let alone children. He addresses these seeming deviations by asserting that "heterogeneity" is a basic property of the human mind. In his view this heterogeneity unfolds developmentally: one form of thinking emerges after and out of another. However, with the appearance of a new form of thinking, previous ones by no means disappear. The result is that his account of the "historic depth" of mind is one of "heterogeneity as genetic hierarchy" (Wertsch, 1991).

In trying to appreciate the broad implications of Subbotsky's arguments, I think it is useful to consider them in the context of other major analyses of heterogeneity, rationality, and irrationality. In particular, I think it is appropriate to consider them from the perspective provided by Ernst Cassirer. Throughout his career Cassirer examined the rational and irrational as they appear in various "symbolic forms" such as language, myth, and science. In his final work, *The Myth of the State*, Cassirer harnessed these ideas in an effort to make some kind of sense out of what was going on in World War II, the scene of what most consider to be the greatest outbreak of virulent irrational forces in the twentieth century. As a German who was at the time living in the United States, Cassirer's struggle to comprehend the dark forces of Nazism was undoubtedly especially painful. In the conclusion to *The Myth of the State* Cassirer wrote:

What we have learned in the hard school of our modern political life is the fact that human culture is by no means the firmly established thing that we once supposed it to be. The great thinkers, the scientists, the poets, and artists who laid the foundations of our Western civilization were often convinced that they had built for eternity . . . It seems, however, that we have to look upon the great master works of human culture in a much humbler way. They are not eternal nor unassailable. Our science, our poetry, our art, and our religion are only the upper layers of a much older stratum that reaches down to a great depth. We must always be prepared for violent concussions that may shake our cultural world and our social order to its very foundations. (1946, p. 297)

Eugene Subbotsky does not attempt to make such sweeping statements about cultural history in *Foundations of the Mind*. His careful theoretical and empirical analyses do, however, have something important and profound to say about what it is to be human, both in a positive and in the all too many negative senses. In particular, by harnessing a host of empirical and theoretical tools in controlled psychological studies he has been able to explicate some of the specific mechanisms that make human rationality neither as eternal nor as unassailable as we often assume.

I write this in the midst of a year's stay in Europe. Over the past several months this continent has witnessed a resurgence in nationalist feelings and hatred that has shocked Europeans as well as the rest of the world. Each day brings news about the horrors of "ethnic cleansing" in the former Yugoslavia, acts of neo-Nazi terrorists in Germany, and other such events. Time and again in the media and in discussions one hears (and says) that we thought we had "moved beyond these kinds of irrational forces." What is most surprising to me, perhaps as an outsider, is the speed and power with which irrational, and in this case virulent forces have arisen after a half century in which they seemed to be largely absent. Unfortunately, Cassirer's warnings about the need to be prepared for "violent concussions" in our cultural world and social order apply today as much as ever.

In this light, the major lasting contribution of Subbotsky's work in *Foundations of the Mind* may be that it provides a few more insights into the complex and dynamic relationship between the rational and irrational sides of human consciousness. He has raised some provocative questions that take us beyond the bounds of normal science in psychology and lead us to reexamine some of our basic and all too complacent assumptions. One can only hope that this turns out to be a contribution to understanding and changing real world practice as well as to academic discourse.

References

Cassirer, E. (1946) *The myth of the state.* New Haven, Conn.: Yale University Press.

Dembo, T. (1967) The dynamics of anger. In J. deRivera (ed.), *Field theory as human science: Contributions of Lewin's Berlin Group.* New York: Gardner Press.

Kaplan, B. (1967) Meditations on genesis. *Human development, 10,* 65–87.

Tulviste, P. (1991) *A cultural-historical approach to the development of verbal thinking.* Commack, N.Y.: Nova Science Publishers.

Wertsch, J. V. (1991) *Voices of the mind: A sociocultural approach to mediated action.* Cambridge, Mass.: Harvard University Press.

Preface

I have been obsessed for a long time with the questions: Why is the world what it is? And what does this mean – to be? No doubt everything we think of exists, but the extent to which the ideas are real varies. Sorcery and witchcraft, which for someone living in Medieval Europe were doubtless realities, have been converted into mere illusions in our rationalistic world. Or have they? The innumerable beliefs people lived with over millennia, where have they all gone? It might be too simple to think they have all disappeared or have become mere illusions of the past. How can a person distinguish what 'really exists' from 'an illusion' in the first place? And what will happen if the illusion suddenly becomes a reality and what we think is real becomes an illusion?

Of course, these questions are as old as the world itself. The attempts to find solutions to them have always been subjects for philosophy, mathematics and logic. Since no philosopher could find a persuasive answer, each individual had to look for the answers him/herself. It is exactly this that seems to be interesting: that what is traditionally considered to be the most complex and difficult, everyone – even a child – has to try systematically to solve individually. The world does not wait until the child becomes mature enough and gets a PhD in Logic. It crashes upon the child from birth with all its complexity and chaotic diversity. And the child has to find what is reliable and real in this disorder, and ignore what is merely an illusion. And the most interesting thing is not *when* the child starts to do this accurately, but *how* the child can do it at all. What do children rely on when there seems to be nothing to rely on?

First, what psychological function could do the job? Thinking? But in order to think, at least to compare two separate things, one already has to have the world populated with stable objects and be able to distinguish between reality and illusion. Memory? But memorizing needs the same. Experience? But for the experience to exist one has to be able to distinguish between a cause and a consequence, and to tell real causes from illusory ones. And despite the fact that the process of attributing reality (or unreality) to things in its mature form includes all these functions, it cannot be reduced to either one of them, or to their mechanical sum.

In my search to find the answers I turned to philosophical tracts. Gradually, I found that a psychological reality which deals with 'attribution of being' exists, and this is consciousness – consciousness not as a mere 'stream' and not as a sum of psychological functions, but as an independent whole with a structure and functions of its own. The basis for consciousness is that without which one cannot imagine 'existence': the ideas of object, causality, space and time. These are the simplest and the most fundamental structures of the mind. One cannot explain them, but they are a necessary condition to explain everything else. They cannot be taught: they simply are. Like our heart contractions, we normally are not aware of them, but if they stop, so does life. They are constantly active, they are mighty pumps, which support the dome of the mind. Try to loosen their action – and reality drastically changes. What used to be 'truth' suddenly becomes an illusion, and what has been an illusion acquires a solid reality. In the new world – the world of transformed consciousness – objects lose their permanence, time can go backwards and magic possesses creative power.

Therefore, the reality of the mind is heterogeneous; it consists of several domains, each having causality, space and time of its own. It includes both what we call usual or 'everyday' reality and what is in no way 'usual': realities of fantasy, dream, pretend play or the fine arts. The individual not only lives in this 'magic sphere', he or she travels within it, passing from one domain to another or sometimes sticking on the border-line. Each time one is confronted with different types of an object, causality, space and time, and with different concepts of what is real and what is fake.

How does this sphere develop? When does everyday reality become separated from the realities of dreams or fairy tales? How do children's concepts of an object, space, time and causality change? Only the answers to these questions can bring us to the solution of the central task: what 'personal criteria' an individual utilizes to endow things with 'reality'. Who has tried to answer these questions? Arguably, Piaget was the first. His *The Construction of Reality in the Child* brought me a genuine pleasure.

This promising start, however, remained uncompleted. Some of the problems were solved, many of them were merely challenged, but the majority were still unanswered. The most difficult task was to believe Piaget when he said that at the age of two the child's practical actions become completely guided by the space and time of everyday reality. Magical causality, for instance, still remains in the domain of verbal judgements, but now it is a mere question of time for our little 'practical rationalist' to become 'a rationalist in theory'. The illusion of magic, after having lost control over the child's practical actions, gradually disappears from the child's judgements.

But what of children's fears, which for many older children are still 'a reality'? And what of adults, many of whom still believe in 'paranormal phenomena' and practise everyday magic and superstitions? Mere observations showed that here was a fascinating field for investigations.

The principle would have to be simple: the person should be given an opportunity to see with his or her own eyes something that was impossible in real life: to witness magic or the spontaneous transformation of one permanent physical object into another one. What would people do? Would they be able to believe that one can stretch one's hand through a glass wall or that an adult can become a little child again? What are the conditions under which the invisible border between everyday and unusual reality dissolves and unusual objects and events permeate real life?

I started a series of experiments in Moscow in 1981. I realized that a contemporary person, familiar with electronic equipment and sophisticated trickery in the cinema and theatrical performances, could hardly be surprised by any complex device. I needed something utterly simple, even primitive.

I remember the thick, wet snow on the streets where I was looking for wood for my first 'magic box'. This simple device could easily turn one physical object into another, could 'swallow' the object without a trace or create the object 'from thin air'. The box started to work. There were many other boxes afterwards. I experimented with nursery school children, with school children, with adults. I continued the experiments in Germany, then in England. Soon, articles in *Soviet Psychology* and *Human Development* appeared. Then this book was created. First, it was a thick volume of 400 pages of Russian text, gradually it turned into what you, my reader, are holding in your hands.

As a result, the developing mind revealed itself as a pulsing dome divided into layers and spheres, and an individual as a traveller in this dome. What makes things complex is that the individual is not 'homogeneous'; he or she lives in two distinct 'planes' of existence – the verbal and the real. In his or her judgements the traveller can be in everyday reality, but his or her real actions may be guided by beliefs in magical causality and in object nonpermanence. The everyday and unusual realities are constantly struggling for dominance. A human being is a 'scene' in which a permanent battle between the everyday and the unusual, between the modern rationalistic and the most ancient 'primitive' beliefs is occurring. In a preschool child the result of the battle is fairly unclear; as the child grows older, the physical causality and the space of everyday reality start to dominate, first in their verbal judgements, and then in their practical actions as well. Under the constant pressure of culture, magical and other anomalous beliefs are being banished to the domains of fairy tales, dreams and fantasies. However, they keep their potency and importance. While periodically crossing the threshold of fantasy and dreams, the individual not only resurrects the feeling of his or her 'ultimate importance' and power, but also 'visualizes' and endows with power special 'ideal objects' which help the traveller to organize and supply with sense his or her ordinary life. There is no logic without imagination; a creator cannot grow from a child who never fantasized and played.

The unusual structures give way, but they do not disappear. It is not desperately hard to create conditions under which a contemporary, educated adult can express belief in magic or object nonpermanence. The ancient gods died, but ancient beliefs flourish. The mind of an individual has its 'historic depth'. Is it not this proximity of the adult's mind to the mind of a child or of 'a primitive' that is responsible for magical and 'paranormal' beliefs? Might it not account for the surprising ease with which twentieth-century myths subordinated the minds of millions, contrary to rational logic? Is it not because of the persistence of unusual, fundamental structures in children's minds that rationalistically-oriented education is such a difficult and time-consuming enterprise? And what is the mysterious underpinning of the fears of children and neurotics if not the ability to attribute reality falsely? Is psychotherapy not a sort of magic in which certain 'unimportant' events in a patient's life are endowed with reality and significance?

I hope this book will be helpful for people dealing with all these problems. It may stimulate interest in specialists on cognitive development and education, in writers and designers of books for children, and in anyone who is not indifferent to the problems of the development of the mind.

Many people contributed to this book either directly or indirectly. Paul Harris recommended the book to Harvester Wheatsheaf and made constructive comments on drafts of various parts of the manuscript. George Butterworth and Farrell Burnett encouraged me to keep working on it and waited patiently. I am grateful to my students who worked with me at Moscow University and to my subjects, both children and adults. My greatest debt is to my wife Luda, to my son Alexej and daughter Natalija, who always were my first and most patient subjects.

Acknowledgements

Chapter 1: this is an abbreviated version of the original Russian manuscript, *Fundament Soznanija. Rasvitije Predstavienij o Realnosti u Rebenka*, translated by Yana Glukhoded. None of the material contained here has previously been published.

Chapter 2: parts of this chapter have appeared in the following journals: 'The preschooler's conception of the permanence of an object (verbal and actual behaviour)', *Soviet Psychology*, 1990, *28*, 3, pp. 42–67; and 'Existence as a psychological problem: object permanence in adults and preschool children', *International Journal of Behavioural Development*, 1991, *14*, 1, pp. 67–82. The material is reprinted with the kind permission of the publishers. The data were also presented by the author in his address, 'Psychological Aspects of Existence', presented at the Third European Conference on Developmental Psychology, Budapest. June 1988; and in 'A life-span approach to object permanence', *Human Development*, 1991, *34*, pp. 125–37. The rest of the chapter is written from material collected recently, during the author's work in Germany (University of Konstanz) and England (University of Lancaster).

Chapter 3: parts of this chapter first appeared as 'Preschool children's perception of unusual phenomena', *Soviet Psychology*, 1990, *28*, 5, pp. 5–24. It is reprinted here with the kind permission of the publishers. Some of the material was presented in the author's invited address 'Phenomenalistic and Rationalistic Perception of the World by Preschool Age Children', at the Fourth European Conference on Development

Psychology, Stirling, 27–31 August 1990. The rest of the chapter contains previously unpublished material collected by the author and his students at the Department of Psychology, Moscow University.

Chapter 4: this chapter is written from material collected by the author in Moscow. It has not been previously published in English. Some of the material was presented in the author's paper 'Early rationality and magical thinking in preschoolers', given at the symposium 'Rationality and Early Reactions to Magic', at the Eleventh Biennial Meeting of the International Society for the Study of Behavioral Development (ISSBD), Minnesota, Minneapolis, USA, 3–7 July 1991.

Chapter 5: this chapter summarizes the previous four chapters and their theoretical discussion and sets it in a broader cultural and philosophical context.

Foundations of the Mind

Chapter 1

The ontogenesis of individual consciousness as a scientific problem

Scientists noted long ago that reality in the child's consciousness in the first years of life, which we interpret by analogy with adult consciousness (and more precisely, with our own consciousness), is global and non-differentiated. Bühler wrote of early childhood as the period of fairy tales, when the child really believes in dwarfs and giants and extraordinary adventures, localizing them in a familiar forest, for instance (Bühler, 1930, p. 342).

Later on, the fairy-tale world is differentiated from the real world and loses its reality for the child. This was also noted by Stern (1923). While developing his idea of the projective significance of unusual reality, Freud showed great interest in infantile dreams, phobias and fantasies. Moreover, he formulated and developed the hypothesis that the basic cause of certain features in the character of an adult could, in fact, consist of the fantasies (complexes) in childhood, which once had been endowed with the status of fully-fledged reality and had left a permanent impression on the personality, irrespective of the following 'deontologization' (Freud, 1966).

At the same time, these studies did not formulate any questions of the structural development of the child's consciousness, due to a lack of experimental data.

The first to study the specifics of the formation of reality in the child's consciousness was Jean Piaget. The results of his work were published in his famous books, *La Naissance de l'intelligence chez l'enfant* (1936), *La Construction de réel chez l'enfant* (1937a), and *La Formation du symbol chez l'enfant* (1937b). Adopting homeostasis as a suitable model for the

1

description of the relation between subjectivity and external reality, he described the development of the infantile intellect as the process of assimilation and accommodation, which attains a dynamic equilibrium at each new stage. However, this model is too general and its explanatory value is doubtful.

The model used by Piaget to describe reality (i.e. individual subjectivity) turned out to be more fruitful on the basis of his observations of children's behaviour. Piaget distinguished and described the features and dynamics of the fundamental structures of consciousness in infants: their representations of an object, causality, space and time.

In the early stages of development, these structures can only result in a chaotic world of 'pictures', which are inalienable from the activity inherent in a child. In the following stages the fundamental structures undergo changes, with the resulting emergence of the world of the 'independent' reality: the world of relatively stable objects, independent of the activity of the child's Ego and located in 'outer' space. But independent reality is still centred in the child and is exclusively 'phenomenal', i.e. it lacks the objective basis in certain 'rational constructions'. The latter appear with the development in the child of the means of symbolic representation of the world (signs and symbols, especially speech), mainly between 18 and 24 months. As a result, the child develops a notion of objective space and time, along with object permanence and physical causality.*

However, these notions exist only in the child's actions (at the level of the sensorimotor intellect); at the level of verbal behaviour the child regresses towards those that are typical of the earlier stages. All subsequent studies on the child's notions of object, time, causality and space have been carried out by Piaget at this representative (verbal) level. Essentially, the majority of Piaget's works, which have earned high acclaim in contemporary science, deal with the development of 'rational constructions' in the child, through which the child obtains the means of verification of the phenomenal world.

First and foremost, these constructions include the concept of conservation (of substance, weight, volume, length, area, etc.), which enables the child to see in the phenomenal world (e.g. in a ball of plasticine) an object endowed with a stable, permanent, essence-weight volume, the

---

* See subsequent chapters for a more detailed description of the fundamental structures in the works by Piaget and other authors.

quantity of the substance (or as Descartes would have termed it certain 'initial qualities'), rather than simply a 'certain object' (Piaget, 1967). Furthermore, these constructions also include the concept of number (Piaget and Szeminska, 1950), the logical operations of classification and serialization (Inhelder and Piaget, 1969), geometric constructions (Piaget and Inhelder, 1963; Piaget, Inhelder and Szeminska, 1948), objective time (Piaget, 1946b), the notions of the motion of bodies (Piaget, 1946a), probability (Piaget and Inhelder, 1951), etc.

The whole of this complex picture is devoted to the development of everyday reality of consciousness in the child. These works of Piaget's generated the fundamental themes in the field of developmental psychology. The process of differentiation of various realities of consciousness in the child has been further elaborated experimentally. First, while studying the development of notions of the world and physical causality, Piaget discovered that in the early stages of representative intellect, judging from the child's answers to specially formulated questions, neither the object nor causality and space can be viewed as 'scientific'. What was even more unexpected, children believe in the direct accessibility of alien consciousness (things 'are aware' of human intentions), in the direct effect of subjectivity upon objects of the outer world (finalism), in non-permanence of objects, in magic causality. Only gradually (by the age of 7–8 years) is the world stripped of all these bizarre structures and does it acquire the features of everyday reality (Piaget, 1927, 1936, 1937a, b). Simultaneously with this, the process of the formation of unusual realities – dreams, imagination and play – is taking place, and was analysed by Piaget in a special study (Piaget, 1937b).

Piaget saw the beginning of the process of differentiation between realities in imitation, which he interpreted as the initial stage of the representation of phenomena in 'internal' form. Emerging in infancy, imitation develops in two directions. On the one hand, after increasingly meeting the objective requirements of people and things, it is gradually converted into 'language' (in the broad sense of the word, to include drawing, the plastic arts, dancing and rituals, rhythms and sounds of speech, script signs, etc.). On the other hand, it engenders the world of inner images, imagination, dreams and plays.

A fundamental feature of the studies by Bühler, Freud and Piaget is that two distinct subjects have been studied in mixed form. On the one hand, it was the study of the development of separate psychological functions (thinking, imagination, symbolic function, etc.), which later gave rise to several independent lines of research. On the other hand, a special problem was raised – the problem of the development of individual consciousness, which was neither one of the functions nor the mechanical sum of them. Rather, it was a peculiar psychological reality, whose independent existence remained an open problem in developmental psychology.

Only in one of his books did Piaget address this problem directly (Piaget, 1937a). However, this line of research was not continued in subsequent studies, save for the elaboration of certain methodological tools (object permanence in particular). The chief subject matter of the book – the development of individual consciousness – remained outside the scope of developmentalists' attention.

At the same time, Piaget's work and its outcome reveal the fact that it is not possible to study the development of consciousness without a certain theoretical analysis of the subject. The absence of such an analysis may produce the impression that the main fundamental structures (that is, the development of object permanence, of spatial and temporal fields and of causality) have been chosen by Piaget arbitrarily, though intuitively correctly.

Indeed, why do the fundamental structures of subjective reality consist only of these intuitive concepts, and not, for instance, of symbolic function or number conservation? What relationship does individual consciousness have to symbolic play, dreams, fairy tales, on the one hand, and to conservation of quantity and language development, on the other? Thus it has become clear that further experimental analysis of the development of consciousness encounters certain theoretical problems: What is individual consciousness as an independent psychological entity? What are its structures, its domains, its functions?

This chapter examines these questions. In so far as this inquiry is not an end in itself but instead serves the reader in understanding the subsequent experimental studies, it will be restricted to a minimum in all those aspects that concern the peripheral sciences (philosophy, logic, etc.). However, it cannot avoid these aspects altogether, for a hyper-reticence here can well make it more difficult to understand the subsequent material.

The fundamental structures of consciousness

We are captured within the limits of subjectivity, and cannot leave its bounds, since anything that penetrates consciousness is tinged by it and is welded into the 'matter of subjectiveness'. At the same time, in spite of the constant and titanic work by our Ego in its attempt to unite the elements of subjectiveness, drawing them together into a single centre and create a harmonious ensemble, this cannot be fully achieved. Something alien, inaccessible to the control of our Ego, 'not created by it', is ever penetrating the tissue of consciousness.

First, what is alien is the physical reality ('outer world') and in particular the elements of it which possess the 'inner', psychic measurement: things are like an irritating ringing invading our minds at inappropriate moments and preventing us from concentrating on something. There is a divine 'subscriber' behind any one thing, whose intentions are known only to us to the extent that it informs us.

An image-ritualized description of these subscribers is the principal element of the religious *Weltanschauung*, from the magic of antiquity to monotheism. In scientific terminology, Kant introduced an effective term, ' a thing-in-itself', to denote the 'subscribers'.

As a result, the sensory image appears as a symbol, a subjective, correlative of the thing itself, as a representative of the external in the world of the internal. How do I know that the film of the subjective image screens 'a thing-in-itself'? How can I tell this image from a pure product of subjectivity: hallucinations and illusions or the stable appearances, which are also independent reality? This can be achieved if we assume that our thinking and synthesizing 'Ego' in some obscure way, incomprehensible in principle, is directly connected with 'the thing-in-itself', outside and beside the prism of subjectivity that mediates this connection. Only such a direct connection can, for instance, explain a multitude of wonderful phenomena; in particular, the phenomenon of the restoring 'sensation of reality' of the outer world in the condition of the distorted prism of subjectivity, which Stratton first encountered (Stratton, 1986; see also Kohler, 1970).

No less mysterious for our Ego is its *'per se'*. We feel it as a power acting within us and creating the structure of reality, but its own origin remains obscure. We recall a name or an idea and feel it as our own, our exclusive possession, but where were the name and the idea before the power acting within us brought them to the surface of consciousness? Whence do we know that it is that very name or that very idea? If we understand something as the truth, where does this 'clarity' suddenly come from? Where does the distinct realization that this is *the truth* come from?

All this is possible on the following condition only: the truth (a name, an idea) was already in our possession. In other words, 'you can understand only that which you have already understood' (Mamardashvili, 1984, p. 12). This is how the sphere of the 'external' is discovered, to which Plato assigned the form of 'knowledge as recollection' of something already seen. Consciousness is directly associated with the divine, is connected with it and recognizes this knowledge as 'the truth'. In contemporary Western tradition, this external foundation and source of subjectivity appears as a 'being', 'the subconscious', 'affordances', etc. How is subjectivity represented? I shall use the term 'fundamental structures of consciousness' to denote the structures that form the basis for subjectivity and that are absolute (not derived from anything). As a rule, a group or a bundle of structures is distinguished and is tautologically interlinked and forms the facets, aspects of a single whole.

First, we clearly feel the effort or the power acting within us (reflected in psychology in such notions as 'needs', 'aspirations', 'motives', etc.), the products of which, although to differing extents, are both dependent, e.g. created and controlled by our 'Egos' and independent reality. This power is granted us directly, and it generates the idea of *duration* as a certain persistence of effort. On the other hand, the reality brought about by effort (sensations, images, objects, etc.) gives us the idea of consistency and alternation. It is noteworthy that this idea already contains the idea of *irreversibility*, the non-equivalence of the elements of consciousness ('A after B' is not equal to 'B after A'). The elements, arranged into sequence, are individualized, distinguished and hierarchically subordinated. The idea of duration and sequence taken together, constitute the idea of *subjective time*.

The structure derived from power and time is that of a permanent object. Essentially, the idea of sequence denotes that, while following one another, events possess a certain duration of existence (or, to put it differently, simply existence), and this duration sets the given events as certain stable integrities, differing from the others (following or preceding them). That which possesses the attribute of constant existence (or simply existence) in subjective reality is called the *object*. In the long run, subjectivity appears to us as a sort of connection, an alteration of stable discrete entities or objects.

Furthermore, the fact that the power acting within us (or the effort we undertake in either active or passive form, acting or simply sensing a requirement) encounters resistance (independent reality) or produces something (dependent reality), contains the idea of causal connection. The connection between the effort and the product that follows it surely exists as a sequence, but it does contain 'something else', namely, the idea of causality. As distinct from sequence, causality is a specific form of the individualization of two events, in which they do not merely follow each other but are linked by a stronger connection, representing a 'transmission of a certain content' from one object (cause) to the other (consequence), or one object engendering the other.

In contrast to the described structures (effort, time, object, causality), in which both dependent and independent reality are represented, there is a structure specific to the sphere of existence, which we refer to as the 'physical world'. This structure is the extent and *expanse (space)*. As distinct from image or thought, the object of sensation and perception exists in space, occupies a certain 'place'.

Attempts to distinguish the fundamental structures date back far in the history of thought. In Antiquity, naive theories of 'subtle matter' (water, air, fire) were replaced by the rather more sophisticated theories of Leucippus and Democritus on atoms and vacuum. Descartes found these structures in 'simple things', reckoning among them the idea of 'figure', 'extension', 'motion' and 'duration'. (Descartes, 1952, p. 21). Locke would speak of 'primitive ideas', which compose a ground for everything. They are the ideas of 'power', 'existence', 'time', 'succession' and 'duration' (Locke, 1961, vol. 1, p. 101). Finally, Kant successfully completed this line of theorizing by formulating the theory of space and time as a priori forms of consciousness in his doctrine on transcendental aesthetics.

The essential feature of this line of thinking is a gradual realization of the special position of the fundamental structures of consciousness, i.e. their fundamental and absolute character, which is principally inaccessible to perception and objective analysis. Democritus' atoms are inaccessible to contemplation due only to the insufficient capacity of the eye; Locke wrote about the impossibility of explaining 'primitive ideas' verbally, and Descartes of an 'inborn' character of 'primitive things'. While withdrawing the question of the inborn or acquired character of fundamental structures, Kant introduced the concept of an a priori form: 'But that in which our sensations are merely arranged, and by which they are susceptible of assuming a certain form cannot be itself sensation. It is, then, the matter of all phenomena that is given to us *a posteriori*; the form must lie ready *a priori* for them in the mind, and consequently can be regarded separately from all sensation' (Kant, 1965, p. 128).

Essentially this indicates the absolute character of the fundamental structures, which, being the basis for the cognition of the 'upper storeys' of subjectivity, cannot be understood themselves. They can only be described indirectly and represented symbolically. An attempt in the modern tradition to treat the fundamental structures as 'inborn' is, in fact, the result of a vicious circle. The very notion of innateness, established in biology in the nineteenth and twentieth centuries, is a product of the development of the concept of the 'physical world', i.e. one of the spheres of subjectivity. The concept of innateness exists within the context of the scientific views on space and the structures of matter, owing to which the idea of a definite 'geometry' of genes, their molecular structure, their role as information carriers, etc., appears. That is why the attempt to limit the concepts of 'a priori knowledge' by these notions is an attempt to derive the cause from the consequence. In essence, a priori forms are no more than postulates in the 'science of subjectivity' and are thus close to the postulates of geometry. Of course, they set the limits for cognition, but only to the degree that such boundaries are a precondition for the existence of any rational system, in particular, natural sciences.

To sum up, object, space, time and causality are the basis of subjectivity. The structures are tightly mutually linked so that it is impossible to talk about one of them (i.e. object) without touching upon the others (space, time, causality). This circle, however, is not vicious, since it links not distinct entities but facets of a single whole – the basis of consciousness.

The spheres of the reality of consciousness

The variety of subjectivity is undoubtedly heterogeneous. We can see that in different periods of time (and sometimes simultaneously) subjectivity functions as if in different regimes. The objects, the means of their interaction, space and time under these regimes, differ from each other to such an extent that only the constancy of our Ego, retaining its identity throughout innumerable transformations from one regime to another, enables us to refer it to one and the same thing, i.e. to our subjectivity.

The first, most capacious and stable regime of functioning is the 'everyday life regime', or, as it is often referred to, 'the regime of normal vigilance'. The characteristic feature of this regime is that within its bounds consciousness is doubled. We think, act, feel, and at the same time *we know* that we think, act and feel. We act while observing ourselves, and hence, base ourselves upon something else other than our Ego, which enables us to interrupt the action or change the purpose of it.

It is easy to see that everyday reality is the reality of individual consciousness, which involves the idea of the 'external' or divine world. The fulcrum we stand upon with a part of our consciousness, and which for all this does not belong to that consciousness, is, in fact, the external, divine consciousness, the creator and guardian of the natural laws, physical properties of the objects, the ideal space and time. We see the physical world and society and our own psyche in the light of these universal laws. That is why the order or 'the prearranged harmony' reigns in the sphere of everyday reality.

As a rule, we find ourselves in everyday reality with the alarm clock. An utterly different reality exists where we were before: the fantastic, chaotic world of our night dreams sometimes obscure and then strikingly bright. The world of events now mirroring our everyday life and then amazing us by its strange and illogical character. Two persons can merge into one, an old person can become young, and vice versa. Objects can change their shape and colour and metamorphose into each other. Of course, even in this strange, quivering world, everyday reality never leaves us alone. We continue to fight our enemies, strive for our goals, fear failure. But in spite of all the boundaries and obstacles, our secret wishes are suddenly realized, while something we had been working so hard to achieve in reality instantly bursts like a soap bubble. Extreme happiness and misery are close in this world. We have only to reach out our hands – here they are! The whole world is woven by our creative fantasy, the product of our wishes, fears and hopes. We only have to think of something and it immediately acquires a visible form. We only have to be scared and the object of our fright, all at once acquiring an illusory reality, is already approaching us. The objects allegedly 'know' and 'feel' our attitude to them, and 'consciously' obey our will or oppose it.

Waking up, we regain once more the stable everyday reality world, the world of strict and stable laws. Momentarily, while waking up from a deep sleep, we freeze in amazement: Who are we? Where are we? What is around us? But the threads of the past and present, as if obedient to a skilful hand, are instantly tied together, and we shrug off the torpor of sleep. Once in its stable bed again, the stream of our life is inexorably flowing forward. We get up, wash, have breakfast and go to work. Everything around us is familiar, natural, ordinary. Even strange phenomena in this world do not surprise us very much, as we are sure they will be studied and explained.

But we are capable of 'falling out' of the everyday reality sphere now and then, even in our active state. While walking along the street or sitting on a bench in the shade of a tree, we are lost in thought and the surrounding world, inspired by our fantasy, is magically transformed. Once again the objects become subject to our wishes and respond to them. And once again obstacles, which seemed insurmountable, vanish into thin air and we hopefully stretch out our hands to our cherished goal. Bizarre images once again crowd in before our eyes. In this world – the world of fantasy – everything is possible.

And what about the world of children's games? How easily do children introduce in their play the adventures of Puss in Boots from the fairy tale! How deftly do they destroy their enemies and counteract the magic charms of an evil wizard. A branch is turned into a charger as if by magic, a slab of wood is a sword and the burdocks by the fence are powerful giants. Of course, children's play is not only the world of fantasy. It subordinates to its own internal laws of play. But these laws have nothing against turning a mitten into a live puppy and allowing a teddy bear to speak with a human voice. Toys and play objects are 'kind' to children. They 'know' and 'feel' what the little dreamers want, and willingly respond to their wishes.

Last but not least, the world of art – poetry, painting, literature. The creative fantasy of the artist cannot limit itself by simply copying the world – it transfigures the world. Both usual and unusual, natural and supernatural, are present in this newly woven world. Poetry awakens objects from their age-old sleep by its divine breath – now they are 'thinking', 'feeling', 'speaking'. They frankly expose their secret souls to the artist. The artist is connected through these secret spiritual ties of 'complicity' and 'co-experience' not only with people: birds and fishes, plants and stones, all speak with him or her. For the poet, the whole world is full of life, soul and as yet obscure consciousness, which is ready to awaken. No doubt fantasy, play and art are the spheres of psychic reality, into which we seldom submerge ourselves fully. We penetrate them, but part of our consciousness is always present in everyday reality, and only a night dream is capable of seizing us completely. But for all their differences, these spheres are united by one thing: unusual, super-natural and incredible events are possible in them. Only in them can objects acquire their soul and consciousness. Nowhere else is the spiritual and material, the psychic and physical not separated by an impenetrable border.

Thus we see that, if globally described (as fantasy, fairy tale, night dreams), unusual reality differs from everyday reality in some respects. First, attributes characterizing the fundamental structures of consciousness are disturbed inside it; there emerges the reversibility of sequence (time), nonpermanence of objects (transfigurations), disappearance of space as a permanent solidity of objects (permeability of the solid bodies), upsetting of physical causality (the direct affect of subjectivity – will power, needs and words upon inanimate material objects). Second, the border separating the psychic from the physical is breached (anomalization of 'inanimate' objects, the capability of animals to reveal human consciousness, speech and human forms of behaviour).

It is not difficult to see that the basis of all these seemingly multifarious differences is one and the same: the destruction (weakening) of the border between dependent and independent realities. Actually, independent reality by definition is not the result of the Ego exclusively, nor, which is practically the same thing, does it have its own internal (psychic) dimension. It is the manifestation of the internal in it ('the thing-in-itself') that guarantees its independence. At the same time its internal is, in fact, the external for us, i.e. what is inaccessible to contemplation. Thus the criterion responsible for independent reality can be formulated as a prohibition: 'internal in things' (including the consciousness of another person or the psychological screen of any living creature) is inaccessible to direct contemplation.

Furthermore, it is evident that, were such contemplation possible at all, it would call for the 'merging of subjectivities', the impossibility of distinguishing 'one's own' from the 'alien' in subjectivity. In other words, while directly contemplating the internal, we could affect it (and thus, the thing *per se* as well) and change it by an effort of our creative thought. In fact, it would mean the transformation of the thing into a dependent reality. But the dependent reality (e.g. an image born in our imagination) is not permanent, it does not consist of 'solid' objects and is not deployed in space and in unidirectional time.

Destruction (or weakening) of the border between dependent and independent realities explains another specific feature of unusual reality – the presence of 'the excessive internal' in inanimate objects and manifestations of consciousness in animals. Whereas the internal of things (i.e. 'the things-in-themselves') becomes 'kindred' to our internal, and, breaking the film of subjectivity, interjects with it directly, a double process is possible: on the one hand, 'the draining' of the 'internal' out of the things, which results in the latter merging with our Egos and turning into a dependent reality – the creature of our consciousness, on the other hand, the transition of the part of the 'Ego's power' inside the external thing and the emergence in it of the excessive internal (as a result, animalization of the inaminate nature, anthropomorphisation of animals, etc.).

From this two opposite but interrelated phenomena result, which are characteristic of unusual reality – 'the creation of the world' by the effort of our Ego only, without the mediating participation of the body, and the animalization of the world, the manifestation of spontaneity of inanimate objects and consciousness in animals. Thus emotionally coloured thoughts and images (e.g. fears), which in everyday reality are easily controlled and suppressed by our Ego, are hypertrophied within unusual reality and acquire visible shape in our night dreams (attack, catastrophe).

Hence while in everyday reality a 'decentred' world is represented, unusual reality is woven out of fragments which are drawn together in one centre – our Ego. The exponent of this 'drawn' state is the fact that under the unusual reality regime the tale of formal logic is substantially decreased. Such concepts as 'the truth', 'objectivity' and 'law' stop ossifying consciousness and the synthesyzing, combinational power of the Ego drastically increases. However, devoid of an external basis, the Ego remains alone. The opposition of the outer world weakens; and thus results in the decrease of order inside subjectivity, into chaos and non–existence. Consequently, what we call unusual reality is an intermediate, marginal state of consciousness in which the border between dependent and independent realities is only weakened but not annihilated.

The levels of behaviour and the planes of representing reality

As well as the spheres of consciousness it might be helpful to distinguish between two distinct levels of functioning of the human individual. Our functioning unfolds at the *involved level* when the reality closely connected with the satisfaction of vital needs (physiological and social) is the object of the activity. This means that our very *being* depends upon the degree to which we manage to assimilate this reality, i.e. to understand, grasp and subordinate it to our control. On the other hand, the reality which is not directly connected with vital needs is assimilated on the *uninvolved level*. Our motivation on the uninvolved level can be quite strong (e.g. when reading a thrilling book), but none the less, our existence depends on the final product of the action in a considerably smaller degree than, for example, on our deeds in a situation of moral conflict or in passing an important examination.

The distinction between these behavioural levels is one of the classical ideas of psychology. Plato expressed his surprise at the non-coincidence of human words and deeds (Plato, 1968, p. 241, etc.). Aristotle opposed reason and sensations: pure reason is independent of wishes and 'is not mixed up with anything'. As for sensations, they depend on wishes and can be stirred by passions (Aristotle, 1976, pp. 433, 434). The opposition between 'clear' and 'dim' consciousness is present throughout the history of thought, e.g. in Spinoza and Descartes, although they are wrongly associated with the separate abilities of the soul (sensation and mind, reason and passions), whereas a person, in fact, acts as a single whole at all levels. As we shall see later, reality, while being assimilated at the involved level, is to a greater extent endowed with being as far as the subject is concerned than the reality represented at the uninvolved level. This seems to be logical since the measure for the being of reality is the being of the Ego.

Introducing the concepts of the levels of behaviour enables us to specify further the various spheres of psychic reality. We see, for example, that in the sphere of everyday reality we can assimilate differently one and the same problem, depending on the level and consequence of the result for us. Apparently, this is the essential feature of a well-known distinction between the ways in which we plan our behaviour in a definite situation (e.g. in a situation of moral conflict) and in which we behave in this situation. In the former case, the behaviour basically develops in correspondence with the 'external', objective logic and laws. In the latter case, it can intentionally or unintentionally deviate from the line dictated by this logic under the threat that otherwise some of our vital needs will remain unsatisfied.

In the sphere of unusual reality, objects and even spheres are differentiated according to the extent of involvement: thus the actions of a person in a state of hallucination or night dreams occur, as a rule, at the involved level, and free fantasy at the uninvolved level. The classification is given schematically in Table 1.1.

Foundations of the mind

Table 1.1 Types of activity of the mind

Levels of behaviour \ Spheres of reality	Everyday reality	Unusual reality
Involved	Act	Hallucination Night dream
Uninvolved	Planning	Fantasy

Let us compare the spheres of reality of consciousness with the planes of representation of reality, which are traditionally distinguished in psychology. They are: a plane of sensory perceptions, a plane of imaginary representations and a plane of symbolic constructions. In all these planes, one and the same event belonging to both everyday and unusual reality can be introduced to consciousness. Thus, an unusual event, contradicting the norms of everyday reality (e.g. a supernatural transformation), may be reproduced as a sensory image (a cartoon), as a product of imaginary representations (imaginary fantasy) or as a product of reasoning (verbal fantasy). The events in the sphere of everyday reality can pass through the same planes of consciousness (Table 1.2).

Finally, there are specific forms of unusual reality, which exist *on the basis* of everyday reality and coexist with it. This is creative fantasy and play. Consciousness bifurcates, existing simultaneously in both regimes of functioning, which enable us to control the products of fantasy to a certain extent. This feature distinguishes these forms of unusual reality from the forms of unusual reality that monopolize consciousness (night dreams, hallucinations) and do not depend upon conscious control.

Table 1.2 Types of representation of events in consciousness

The planes of consciousness \ Spheres of reality	Everyday reality	Unusual reality
Perception	Perception of 'normal' events (e.g. a mechanical push)	Perception of unusual events (a cartoon, fine arts)
Imaginary representation	Imaginary planning of normal events	Imaginary fantasy
Symbolic representation	Logical (verbal) modelling	Verbal fantasy (autistic thinking)

The properties and functions of the spheres of reality of consciousness

Since the basic reality (the sphere) of consciousness is 'consciousness *per se*', it has no functions. There are certain reasons for assuming that in the contemporary European tradition the basic reality is everyday reality. The only aim of an individual within everyday reality is merely 'life itself', plus development. The remaining spheres of consciousness (e.g. dreams) access their functions with respect to this aim: from the total uselessness (a theory of dreams as a chaotic projection of the irritations of the sense organs at the subjective screen) up to the role of arranging everyday reality itself.

The *first function* of unusual reality most frequently distinguished *is the materialization of unrealized wishes*. According to this view, a considerable part of needs and wishes cannot be satisfied within the framework of everyday reality because of its rigid and internally prearranged structure. Since unusual reality is free of these limitations, the materialization of wishes occurs in it.

Freud introduced the term 'psychic reality' to designate the unusual reality of dream and neurotic fantasies (Freud, 1922).* One of the most important functions of dreaming, in Freud's view (following Scherner, Volkelt *et al.*), is the sublimation of wishes 'banned' in everyday life and forced out into the subconscious (Freud, 1924). This function is particularly clearly demonstrated in children's dreams, which are of a realistic character and are structured as the direct satisfaction of unrealized needs.

The *second function is a projective one*. To demonstrate this function, Freud used verbal fantasy (the method of free association) – the sphere of reality, unbound by logical ties and stereotypes of everyday life. In Freud's view, dreams and neurotic fantasies are projective as well.

It is noteworthy that Freud, who recommended his readers to subject their dreams to analysis for the sake of self-cognition, connected the projective function of dreams with the function of 'the omen', which was

---

* My use of the term 'the reality of consciousness' differs from the term 'psychic reality' as the contents of the former do not boil down to the psychic sphere only, but include also the physical and social worlds.

typical in the consciousness of antiquity (Freud, 1924). Because in dreams (and other spheres of unusual reality) the secret contents of the mind are revealed, the connection is clear, as the contents undoubtedly contribute to human behaviour.

The *third principal function* of unusual reality is in creating and maintaining certain specific objects, which have no analogies in the real world. These are collective and individual fantasies, which have gained the status of reality in myths, religion, children's fantasies and play. And whereas the logical correlates corresponding to these objects – the famous Kantian regulative ideas of the world, God, subject, the ideal objects of science ('ideal gas', 'ideal mobile') – being devoid of anything analogous in the phenomenal sphere, still belong to everyday reality of consciousness, the imaginary representation of these ideas is only possible in unusual reality. 'God', 'beauty', 'good' exist in the individual consciousness not as 'the logical ideas of reason', but as the real characters of a fairy tale, a myth or an *objet d'art*. Outwardly useless, they organize everyday reality, outline the scale for the subject according to which the things, deeds and thoughts find their place in everyday reality.

This *constructive* or organizing function of unusual spheres of consciousness, neglected by the founding fathers of rationalism, found its underpinnings in works on the history of religion, theory of art and children's play. For children, the interrelationships between fairy tale characters, their features ('a good fairy', 'an evil wizard') are not just 'examples', but 'the measures'. It is we who are most probably 'the characters' of the everyday life and 'the examples', particular cases of evil and good, weakness and power. The characters of a fairy tale do not reflect the world, but through their elements of something illusory, invisible, they *construct* the world. If you restrict a child and do not let him play and fantasise, i.e. dwell in something outside experience and life, and have nothing to do with it, he will not grow into a human being (Mamardashvili, 1984, p. 61).

Finally it is possible to distinguish *the fourth 'resurrecting' function*: in the sphere of unusual reality a person can experience a state of ecstasy, the feeling of supreme harmony, completeness, perfection, a direct link to the world. In the sphere of everyday reality such a state is impossible, as we are separated from the world by a film of organised subjectivity, and the world appears to us as 'alien' and 'external'. In the view of A. S. Arseniev, the overcoming of this separation, the sensation of a direct connection with the world, with the infinite, emerges in the state of religious ecstasy, catharsis, mystical contemplation, aesthetic perception or narcotic delirium (Arseniev, 1980).

It may be assumed that when we plunge into the sphere of unusual reality (fantasy, dream, play), thus liberating ourselves from the restrictions of space and time, from being projected to a local, empirically limited spot of existence, we gain a sense of freedom, the feeling of power and omnipotence. While breaking free of the framework of the implacable cyclic monotony of everyday reality, we periodically resurrect the necessary sense of our value and significance.

The structure of everyday reality

It is generally assumed that children's structure of subjective reality substantially differs from adults'. Thus, according to Piaget, the subjective world of a newborn child for the most part is the product of the child's Ego, the dependent reality (*tableaux*) which exists only thanks to the continuous effort of the child's mind (soliptic world). At a more advanced age, part of the power of the child's Ego is alienated from it, as if it were 'forcing its way' into objects, imparting them to independence and individuality. In this world the a priori forms already appear in a quite recognizable form: this is the world of stable objects, existing within space and time and connected by causal interrelations (egocentric world).

However, a specific feature of this universe is that it is centred on the child's Ego. Alienated from the Ego by independent reality, objects are still connected with the Ego as with its foundation: the Ego remains the only foundation and scale, fixing the 'seams' of the world. This is why every object in this world is, in a sense, unique, it has no prototype outside itself. In contrast to the egocentric world, which is changing and diverse, the decentred world of an adult is relatively stable and unchanging: the whole of its empirical variety is driven to its prototypes, which, in their turn, are directly accessible to our mind. In Antiquity, the search for these prototypes can be found as far back as the theory of primary 'origins' in the atomism of Epicurus and Democritus. They are classically embodied in the teaching of 'ideas' by Plato. Essentially, Plato's 'ideas' are 'prototypes', 'rational constructions' of the objects of a certain class, which were, however, regarded by Plato himself not only as a product of the effort of the mind, but as independent foundations, existing outside it.

It is important to note that although 'an idea' is distinguished by analysis through the comparison and correlation between external phenomenal objects (*ratio*), it is not a result of a formal logical generalization or 'abstraction of the general features'. On the contrary, in the 'idea' *per se* (e.g. the idea of beauty) there can be not a particle of what composes the material body of the objects, and for all that, it still expresses their essence. The idea is a 'constructive machine', producing objects of a certain type, but not necessarily resembling them, just as a machine-tool does not look at all like the details it produces.

One of the variations of ideas belonging to the physical world (i.e. the component of the subjectivity existing in space) is a model, in particular a number. Let us consider two subjects, whose phenomenal worlds contain a certain object (let it be a cube). The element of subjectivity caused by the effect of this object on two different consciousnesses can be entirely different, but if it is 'measured' by another object (provided that certain measuring procedures are observed), the resulting relation (number) will be the same.

Thus by means of a model, the variety of the phenomenal world is withdrawn and an equivalent emerges which is invariant in relation to various consciousnesses. A number (denoting length, width, height, etc.) characterizes not the phenomenon but the object *per se*, which is one and the same for all. However, as we know, the object itself is inaccessible to contemplation. Hence the model characterizes the 'external', outside limits of subjectivity, and in this sense an absolutely stable object. Let us call this model 'a rational construction'. It is well known that rational constructions in modern science were created for almost all phenomenal properties of physical objects: size (length, width, volume), weight (mass), external appearance (geometrical shape), colour (the theory of 'waves'), odour (molecular theory), sound (wave theory of sound), etc.

Rational constructions exist for the description of the phenomena of space (absolute physical space), time (objective time), causality (physical causality) and object (physical object).

As a result, the whole phenomenal world within decentred space is 'duplicated'; its second layer is the layer of rational construction or 'essences'. The essences characterize the outer world, the world independent of the individual consciousness, the world of the 'things in their own right'. It is worthwhile recalling once more that rational construction is not 'the thing-in-itself' but its indirect description, and, what is more, it is historically changeable. For all that, everything we know of the 'things themselves' we can learn only through the phenomena and their relations. The historical process of the distinction of essences is, in fact, the process of the moulding of everyday reality of consciousness.

Rational constructions (essences, logical schemes, mathematical and physical theories of various processes, etc.) emerge as the methods of description of the object as it exists in the outer world. The latter thus appears in consciousness twice: in the form of a sensory image (phenomenon) and in the form of a mental rational construction (Figure 1.1). It is evident that the relation between the two types of 'presentation' (rational construction and phenomenon) is one of correlation, and not that between cause and effect.

The fact that the relationship between a phenomenon and its rational construction is a correlational and not a causal one is very important, since it is just this distinction that is crucial for the definition of what can and what cannot be posited as a scientific problem. Let us assume, for instance, that pebbles are splashing periodically in a basin filled with water, producing a rain of drops and sounds. For a child who is below the water surface and cannot observe the falling pebbles it might seem that drops are being produced by sounds. There is, of course, nothing problematic in this misunderstanding unless the interrelationships between drops of water and sounds are put as a scientific problem, that is to determine causal relations. But if it is, it may produce very strange paradoxes, since sounds and drops of water depend upon the shapes and weights of the pebbles in a dissimilar way.

Ignoring this fact leads to 'fundamental incomprehensibilities' in psychology. One such classical 'incomprehensibility' is that of the correlation between the corporeal and the spiritual (the psychophysical connection), which I have already analysed (Subbotsky, 1983). In this chapter I shall dwell on

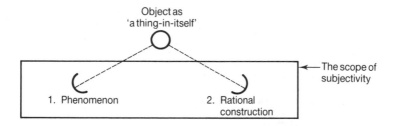

Figure 1.1 The scheme of interrelationships between phenomena and rational constructions

the incomprehensibilities of a different sort, which emerge in the sphere of perception. These incomprehensibilities include, for instance, 'the problem of the third dimension' (why is the visible image three-dimensional despite the fact that the projection of the object on the retina is two-dimensional? (see Hochberg, 1971), and the problem of the constancy of perception (Gregory, 1980). Essentially, these problems are, in fact, caused by surprise at the non-coincidence of the 'distal' and the 'proximal' stimuli.

The image on the retina is (1) two-dimensional, (2) inverted, (3) diminishes with distance quicker than does the 'phenomenal size', (4) moves with the motion of the eye, whereas the 'visible world' remains immobile, (5) receives more light at the sight of a polished coal than a paper, whereas we perceive the coal as black, and the paper as white. In other words, what we actually see is quite different from what is reflected on our retina, and these non-coincidences are very often put as scientific problems.

As a rule, attempts to solve these problems are theoretical constructions, enabling us to explain, for example, how the brain makes up for the lack of information on the retina. (For a review of these problems, see Gregory, 1980.) However, it is evident that the very formulation of these problems (as problems and not mere statements) is based on the prerequisite of the existence of the causal connection between retinal image and the phenomenon. It is presumed that an individual sees the phenomenon while deciphering the retinal information; moreover, the latter is the cause and the visible object is the consequence.

In actual fact, things are quite different.

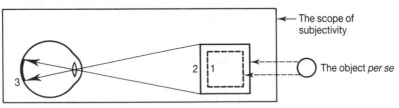

1. Phenomenal image of the object
2. Rational construction of the object (distal stimulus)
3. Rational construction of the retinal projection of the object (proximal stimulus)

Figure 1.2 Relationships between phenomena and rational constructions in visual perception

We can see in Figure 1.2 that there are three, not two, components in the explanation of the act of perception: (1) the phenomenon *per se* (visible size, shape, colour, taste, odour, etc.); (2) the rational construction of the object (the object of a definite size, shape, weight, etc., fixed by measurement); (3) the retinal projection. The components are principally heterogeneous: the phenomenal image is a sensory event, and as for the rational construction and the retinal projection, these are intellectual schemes. In other words, the dynamics of the retinal projection, which is itself a product of rational schemes (disparity, convergence, fusion, etc.), depends upon the rational construction of the object, but the phenomenal image represents 'the object *per se*' as it is given through the film of subjectivity. Thus the phenomenal dynamics (e.g. size) cannot be the consequence of the dynamics of the retinal projection or the dynamics of the object's rational construction, but can only correlate (or not correlate) with the latter.

A prohibition on the direct accessibility of an alien subjectivity constituting the everyday reality of consciousness also testifies to the impossibility of the 'causal transformation' from a retinal projection to a visible image. Both the rational construction and the retinal projection exist within physical space; they can be measured, but the phenomenal image exists in the subjective space of the observer and is principally inaccessible to direct external estimation.

I have already stated that the measure and methods of its application are means of universalization of the phenomenal world, the means of transition to the intersubjective world of the rational constructions. We measure not what we see, but what we *know*. That is why the cube we have measured remains unchanged, whereas its visible size changes with the changing position of our body. That is why the observer, after acquiring the measure and applying it, immediately falls out of the phenomenal subjectivity sphere into the space of rational constructions, including retinal projection. Thus the formulation of the *fact* of the constancy of perception as 'a problem' is fraught with the error of combining the phenomenal and rational spaces.

None the less, this does not mean that it is impossible to compare the rational construction of an object and its phenomenal image (shape, size, colour, odour, etc.). Such a comparison is possible provided both rational construction and phenomena are present in one and the same consciousness, and are elements of *one* subjectivity which reflects the same external object with the help of a different means. But the correlation between what we see (for instance, a decrease by one-third with remoteness) and what we know (the three-fold decrease of the retinal projection) does not appear as a problem, but as a *fact*, requiring a mere statement and a correlational empirical analysis, but not explanation.

Independence of the subjective image (visible world) from the retinal projection is well demonstrated within the framework of the ecological approach to perception (Gibson, 1979). Gibson rejects the orthodox theory of the retinal image, which implicates the idea of 'homunculus in the brain'. According to him, it is not abstract ('value-free') objects only that subjects perceive, but also values (affordances) of things for others as well as for themselves. The information about 'affordances' comes to the subject 'directly' through 'invariants', which a changing optic array contains. The affordance can be misperceived, as in the *visual cliff* experiment, in which the optical information about the depth-downward-at-an-edge is still present in the ambient light while the real danger of falling is prevented by a sturdy sheet of plate glass (Gibson and Walk, 1960). While the idea of 'affordances' which are 'neither physical nor phenomenal' is innovative, the theory of 'invariants' seems to keep all traces of a classical rational construction.

The only plausible solution to the question of the connection between the phenomenal image and the object is postulating that the person and external object are *directly* connected with one another. Subjectivity, a subject and the external have 'a contact point', which results in the emergence of the subjective image corresponding to the 'object *per se*'. As I have already noted, this connection is postulated in various theories by the terms 'subconscious', 'prearranged harmony', 'direct perception of affordances'. Since this connection is a direct one between subjectivity and the external, it cannot be the subject for cognition.

Consequently, everyday reality of consciousness is a 'dual' reality (perhaps even 'triple'): first, the reality of the phenomena *per se* (the sensory images and the fundamental structures typical of this reality – space, time, causality), in which the objects of the outer world appear to us; second, the reality of the rational constructions of the same objects (essences, schemes, models, etc.); and third, the rational constructions of the images *per se* (the schemes and models of perception existing in psychology and physiology: retinal projections, the stream of light, the mechanism of vision, of nervous system, etc. (see Figure 1.2).

It is essential to stress that the phenomenal stratum of subjective reality is neither a consequence of the object's rational construction nor of the rational construction of the phenomenon *per se*. As for the rational constructions, they are a means of description both for the external world and for the world of phenomena. As rational constructions exist in a form of supersensory reality, which is, nevertheless, represented through their visible correlates – signs – we now enter the realm of everyday reality which is called 'psychic'.

The psychic or superphenomenal world represents the part of our subjectivity which exists as a system of objects that are mutually connected in time but are devoid of *extent*, or space. These entities represent dependent reality and owe their existence and stability exclusively to our Ego. However, these entities are still indirectly connected with the external world. This connection is mediated by a *sign* or *name*.

Plato asked how the ideal world of objective creatures (*aidos*) could be assigned to an individual human consciousness. The answer is: with the help of language or a name. The name represents the 'idea', and, at the same time, is an element of the consciousness of an individual human being. For all this Plato stressed the very conditionality of the connection 'idea-name'.

Since each sign can correspond to an infinite number of referents, the retention of the meanings and their interconnections is a specific task for an individual: the job of the assimilation and preservation of languages and of all sorts of rational constructions. This work of our mind makes up the psychic world, or, to be more precise, a section of the psychic, organized in accordance with the laws of everyday reality.

A characteristic feature of this section is *order*: the constancy of the connections between signs and their referents. Whereas in the phenomenal sphere this order is secured by the direct effect of the outer world, in the sphere of the psychic world it requires the active ('distinguishing') effort by the subject and, when this effort lags (dreams, fantasy, madness), the order is instantly upset. As a result, the subjectivity transfers into the regime of unusual reality.

Unusual reality: its structure and types

With the relaxation of the distinguishing effort of the mind, structures appear which are built on the basis of everyday reality's analogies. They are comprehensible and reproducible, although they often strike us with their oddity. The origin of these structures is quite evident: with the weakening of the distinguishing effort, the symbolic ties supported by this effort are broken up; the variety of alternative combinations of symbols and referents, which were previously rejected by this effort, begins to reveal itself. The stable groupings of images, the system of logical ties, are 'dismantled'; the logic-trodden channels of thinking are broken down; however, the destruction is not total.

As a result there appears a peculiar *mixture of fragments* of the fabric which used to compose the 'body' of everyday reality. Still retaining some threads of the referent connections, these fragments of symbols and images are now none the less extracted from the integral context of the phenomenal fabric or thinking process and, simultaneously, due to their 'incomplete senselessness', retain 'valency' – the ability to form new groupings and chains. The fabric of unusual reality is woven out of this unique material (let us call it a 'continuum of fragments').

It is essential to note that in this condition not only are the 'upper storeys' of the symbolic destructured, but the fundamental structures (object, space, time, causality) as well. The prohibitions whose observation was determined by these structures in the sphere of everyday reality now cease to be obligatory: 'the instability of objects' emerges as well as the 'reversibility of processes', 'permeable solid bodies' appear, just as do magic influences and spontaneous upsurges in the animated objects' activity. But let us recall once more that this is not a *total* process: there is no complete destruction of the order leading to non-being. Typical of the unusual fabric of consciousness is its marginality, a combination of usual and unusual chains and symbols.

A transition from everyday reality into unusual reality can occur spontaneously (for instance, an unstable state between sleep and alertness), or intentionally. This enables us to distinguish between spontaneous and non-spontaneous types of unusual reality of consciousness.

Spontaneous unusual reality

A monstrous object, integrally combined out of various components of certain phenomenal images of everyday reality, or a symbol endowed with an unusual referent address, or a connection between objects that contradicts the logic of everyday reality – all this may become *spontaneous* *unusual reality*. In the phenomenal sphere unusual reality is formed under specific conditions, standing in the way of normal perception (a distant location of the object, intransigence of the milieu, malfunctioning of the sensory organs). This is how 'incredible figures' emerge – sensory images whose structure contradicts their rational constructions.*

A vivid example of the work of visual perception in unusual reality occurs when an optical device is worn which inverts the visual field in depth. Since no complete transreal transition occurs, the inversion of the objects whose transformed image is entirely contradictory to their rational structure (e.g. a living human face) does not take place; it nevertheless does occur under certain conditions provided the contradiction is not so great (a plaster mask of a face) (Gregory, 1980).

In the latter case the resulting image is more often than not a compromise between the inverted perceptual image of the object and its 'normal image': if we drape a part of an arm, the observer 'sees a phantasmagoric picture: the part of the arm from the hand to elbow turns into a sort of a gutter paved with something resembling human skin, and on one end this gutter is transformed into a live human hand!' (Stolin, 1976, p. 112). Under these conditions we can witness an upheaval of the usual properties of physical objects and physical space: the objects while being discrete in everyday reality, can merge into a single one (upsetting of the permanence of the object), solid objects acquire the properties of liquids, and vice versa (the transgression of the border between the permeable and impermeable bodies). If a subject is looking at a distant screen through a hole in a near one, the visible part of the distant screen does not 'hang' in front of the near one; rather it merges with the latter, forming a prominence. If a plate with liquid is subjected to inversion, the liquid is perceived as a solid body located on the surface of the inverted plate. A pencil placed on the back of a porcelain elephant at one end and on the top of a cone nearby at the other 'cuts' the back of the elephant and pierces through it, going under the surface of the table after the inverted summit of the cone (Stolin, 1976, p. 191).

Unnatural chains of this kind occur in the image-symbolic aspect as well, bringing about slips of the tongue or the pen, for instance where either the integration of fragments belonging to different symbols

---

* The drawings by Escher, the well-known Dutch graphic artist, are good cases of such objects.

(words, images), or the application of the referent tie of one symbol to another one takes place (Freud, 1966). Whereas artificially-created 'monsters' of pseudoscopic sight are merely curious occurrences, the spontaneous combinations of symbols have projective burdens as well, appearing as a sort of 'window into the subconscious' and supplying an analyst with information about the patient's needs and attitudes, which cannot find expression in the language of everyday reality.

An almost complete transreality transition, occurring in the state of violent emotion and resulting in a desperate situation in delirium or fainting, reaches its rather less dramatic climax in a dream. Since in a dream one loses contact with everyday reality, the dream is approaching the latter with respect to the status of being. As Aristotle noted, there is no method of establishing whether we are sleeping or awake, since we are completely involved in each of these realities (Aristotle, 1952, pp. 530–1).*

Freud distinguished a number of specific features separating dreams from everyday reality. The axis of the *covert* content of a dream consists in the 'materialization' of wishes, which cannot be carried out in real life. None the less its *actual* content (i.e. something that can be reproduced in everyday reality as a recollection) is liable to transformations: condensation (integration of a number of discrete objects into one object), displacement (ascribing significance and value to the objects devoid of it in actual fact and devaluation of truly valuable ones), rapprochement in time and space (a constant connection of objects separated by time and space in the everyday reality), transformation of one object into another (Freud, 1924). These observations clearly indicate a reality based on changing properties of fundamental structures: here the principal prohibitions of everyday reality are violated (a ban on the direct transformation of independent reality in accordance with the wishes of the individual, object permanence, time irreversibility, physical causality). In the total account, the actual material of a dream becomes projective, encyphered information of the dream's covert content. Let us take note, however, that this reality does not tell us anything of the *outer world* – 'nature and society' – limiting itself by the inner world (needs, effects and emotions).

---

* This particular fact served the foundation for a series of logical riddles (Smullyan and Raymond, 1982).

Unspontaneous unusual reality

Basically, this type of unusual reality includes the reality of imagination and of artistic creativity. As far as its outward shape is concerned, the reality of the imagination does not differ significantly from the reality created by a dream or hallucination. Like spontaneous reality it is built from a continuum of fragments, based on fundamental structures with unusual properties, and can 'restore or think up the most incredible combinations of things and distinguish objects which are undistinguishable in reality' (Bacon, 1968, p. 315).

Thus in Clifford Simak's 'Goblin Preservation' and 'All Flesh is grass' we encounter the whole of the familiar set of disturbed fundamental structures: the direct perception of an alien subjectivity (telepathy), the direct effect of subjectivity on the objects of the outer world (the magic and witchcraft of the trolls), the reversibility of time (the reality of a time-machine, transporting objects into the past, the extraordinary abilities of the artist Lambert), object nonpermanence (the transformation of 'flowers' into other objects), the loss of materiality (the transference of material objects within the physical space with infinite velocity) – and extraordinary events derived from them (the animation of inanimate objects, violation of the general logic of everyday reality by way of introduction of unusual creatures: inhabitants from other planets, artificially created animals, dwarfs, dragons, etc.).

Besides, the spheres of functioning of these unusual structures are principally limited and interwoven into the fabric of everyday reality: so sorcerers and magicians are only able to transform certain objects, and to read minds one needs special instruments ('spectacles'), transfer in space is possible only with the help of a special machine etc. In other words, the local character of the manifestations of unusual fundamental structures, their incompleteness, guarantees the presence of a certain structure in the fantastic world, which makes this world sensible and accessible to the perceptions within everyday reality.

We can see similar local shifts of boundaries between the dependent and independent realities in fairy tales and myths. However, along with common features for both the non-spontaneous and spontaneous unusual realities, there is an essential difference: if the function 'materialization of suppressed wishes', the 'projective' and 'resurrective' functions can be attributed to both types of unusual realities, the *'constructive' function pertains entirely to non-spontaneous unusual reality*.

In science fiction objects such as a perpetuum mobile, time machine or a spaceship with infinite velocity are endowed with real being. All these objects are in no way the result of assembling the elements of everyday reality; they exist in the sphere of everyday reality as 'maximal constructions', 'regulatory ideas' (a Kantian term), drawing together all the multiformity of reality into a single whole, setting its scale and measure. In fantasy or myth 'ideal objects' are visualized, transformed into a tangible form, accessible to all human beings.*

In other words, whereas the structures of spontaneous unusual reality only *express*, the structures of non-spontaneous reality *construct* and materialize the world of the possible. Thus children by playing construct abilities not inherent in them within everyday reality. It is not simply suggested here that within pretend play children can exercise certain functions (perception, memorizing, etc.) better than in classroom activity (see El'konin, 1978). What is really important is the feeling of *infinite* power and *infinite* capacities that the child can experience in play. Neither of the existing theories of the origin of children's games can account for the presence of this tendency towards the magical and 'maximal' transpassing of the limits of everyday reality in role play.

An artistic image is endowed with constructive power as well. In the artistic reflection of the outer world features are present that are inaccessible to perception or rational thinking, inexpressible by means of ordinary language, but are *really present* in the infinite multiformity of the external. That is why, despite an artistic reflection having very little in common with either the phenomenal image or the rational construction of the object, it is not in fact 'a distortion' of the object's properties (as is the case in the artificially created world of 'inverted sight'), but, on the contrary, a way of expressing its new properties.

Thus, non-spontaneous unusual reality does not only create objects and fulfil a constructive role with respect to everyday reality, it also enriches everyday reality, introducing in it the properties of the outer world which are absent from the language of everyday reality *'per se'*.

---

* So in the fine arts infinity can be featured through finite special objects such as a dot drawing together a perspective (Arnheim, 1954).

Existentialization as the work of consciousness

The wealth and variety of subjectivity that unfolds before us in the course of even a superficial analysis, in which we cannot trace any absolute boundaries separating one area of subjectivity from other ones, has a specific order, none the less. It is absolutely clear that different elements of subjectivity are not equivalent in value and are strictly hierarchical.

A paradox consists in the fact that, in a certain form, everything exists. But while it is evident that everything exists, it exists in different ways. Some of it exists in the status of notion, other parts exist as phenomena, still others as symbolic images. Some can be true, others false, still others problematic, etc. To bring this diversity into a certain order is an ultimate requirement for individuals, even if they have but poor knowledge of 'logical verification'. This is a necessity of everyday life, and it demands special work: hierarchization of the elements of subjectivity according to the status of being and truth. I shall call this work '*the work of existentialization*' (the attribution of existence).

It is known that there are recognized methods for confirming truth in science: logical deduction and experiment. But this is, in fact, existentialization in its superior, most developed form. As for the elementary forms, the effort of existentialization along with the 'distinguishing' effort are included in any conscious act. Independent of age and level of cognitive development, all individuals in everyday practice have to answer certain questions: What is true and what is false? What exists in reality and what appears only to us? Existentialization answers these questions; it is a specific work of consciousness, which is relevant to consciousness as a whole, rather than to certain individual psychological functions.

It is not my purpose here to address the huge problem of the interrelationships between truth and reality; however, I must touch upon it to the extent that it concerns the everyday work of individual consciousness.

It is obvious that in the world of the infant one can talk only of the comparison between images and phenomena. In the world of older children and adults the situation grows more complicated. The reproduction of the world in the form of rational constructions enables us to verify the phenomena themselves by contrasting them to the corresponding rational constructions (e.g. a contrasting produced detail to the parameters, specified on its technicl diagram). In the total account, the phenomena in

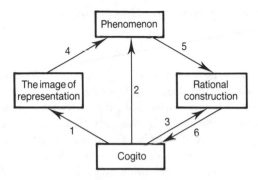

Figure 1.3 A scheme of the relations of existentialization

their turn are subdivided in accordance with the statuses of being. Those among them that correspond to their rational constructions become 'the true', actually existing (e.g. if the visible size of a house exceeds the size of the hand, the relationship between the visible objects is considered as the true one, since it corresponds to the relationship between the metrical measurement); those that contradict rational constructions are considered false (the visible size of the hand is bigger than the house located farther away). Owing to the mutability of phenomena and the stability of rational constructions, the latter acquire the status of the 'genuinely existing', 'the essence', the phenomena boil down to the status of 'the appearance' or a secondary reality.

At the same time rational constructions '*per se*' possess the basis for verification, and this base is 'obviousness': the rational construction, the 'model', is true for me if its existence is as obvious for me as my own existence ('cogito'). As a result, all three forms of being of any element of subjectivity are connected with each other by the relations of existentialization (Figure 1.3). The relations 1, 2 and 3 only ascertain that any element of subjectivity is present in consciousness and is endowed with being at the lowest level – the level of dependent reality. In other words, although each of them exists, it can be a pure product of consciousness.

The relations 4, 5 ad 6 are the relations of existentialization specifying the existential status of the given element, i.e. determining whether the image, the phenomenon or the rational construction is false or true. Respectively, elements of subjectivity, which could not withstand the test for genuine reality, are endowed with a 'weak' (or 'incomplete') being; the elements ascribed with the truth are endowed with a 'strong being'.

The status of being of external objects can now be described. For instance, the weakest status of being is usually ascribed to the element that exists only in one possible form: as an image, a phenomenon or a rational construction. Thus, a fantastic ('Kentaurus') image or an extinct species of animal may exist in consciousness but cannot be reproduced alive through scientific methods. Purely rational constructions (such as the 'ideal mobile') devoid of any analogues in the real world are not endowed with the completeness of being as well. The same status is assigned to a pure phenomenon, e.g. a stable illusion of perception. Especially convincing is the false nature of certain artificially created figures, e.g Escher's 'an incredible triangle'; each of them exists in the phenomenal field, but any attempt to erect its rational construction proves to be futile.

However, if an object exists in the consciousness as an image, a phenomenon and a rational construction simultaneously and all these forms correspond to each other, this object possesses the maximal completeness of being, or *actual being*. Usually we simply say that the object 'really exists'.

So the statuses of being of an external object can be endowed in consciousness with the actual (strong) or incomplete (weak) being. It is evident that this 'endowment' is flexible: the object with incomplete being can acquire actual being, if any referents for it are found in the real world or if its rational construction is created; in particular, the work of scientific and technical fantasy is normally the initial stage in this process, when objects are initially created as images and then as rational constructions and phenomena.

At the same time, one cannot exclude the possibility of false existentialization, the assignment of the status of potential or even actual being to objects devoid of these criteria. Whereas such errors can be purely 'theoretical' at the uninvolved level (e.g. a scientific error or a mistaken identification of a person), at the involved level it can be grave enough (of which the errors in politics or social life are the most vivid manifestations, along with blind faith in the true nature of the constructed models of 'the best' social system, or, on the contrary, the discounting of danger when controlling sophisticated technological equipment).

Examples of the disturbed mechanisms of existentialization are various forms of fanaticism, faith not informed by reason or hallucinatory states in the case of mental illness. In some cases there is an erroneous 'intensification' of the subjective phenomena's 'reality', while, in other cases, one can witness its weakening. A derealization of this kind can be experienced by people who have lost their sight and both hands: 'It was as if I was only reading about things, not seeing them . . . the things were farther and farther' (this is a description of his state by an amputee, who had gone blind. He complained that when somebody greeted him he felt 'as if there were nobody') (Leontiev, 1977, p. 136).

The study of existentialization in children

In studies by Freud and Piaget unusual spheres of reality were regarded as 'immature' forms of consciousness or as the 'background' and 'facilitator' of the development of everyday reality. While critically assessing this approach, Vandenberg (1983–4, 1985) proposed the idea of regarding reality as the creation of myths through which people order their experience and endow it with meaning. Hence the re-estimation of the role of children's fantasy play: while playing, children create imaginary worlds which help instil structure, vitality and meaning into their experience (Vandenberg, 1983–4). Thus, it is fantasy, rather than logic and science, which is the initial element of adaptation and organization of the world.

A similar point of view is voiced by Krippner, when speaking of the functions of dreams (Krippner, 1986). He believes that the dream is, in fact, a method of creating personal myths – specific cognitive structures, moulding perception, thinking, emotions and behaviour. Dreams supply new experience to the structure of new and old personal myths.

Such a theoretical re-estimation of the role of unusual realities sheds new light on experimental studies of the process of distinguishing between the realities. In particular, at what age and why does the child divide objects into real and fantastic ones? Thus, Morison and Gardner gave children some drawings of objects to classify, with some of the drawings representing fictitious prototypes and others real ones (Morison and Gardner, 1978). It turned out that the older the children were (children aged between four and twelve years took part in the experiment) the more capable they were of distinguishing between symbols of fantastic objects and symbols of real ones. But the ability to ground the differences through application of the status of being of the prototypes ('borrowed from a fairy tale', 'invented') increased but slowly by the age of eleven.

Yet the question of the reasons why children designate certain objects as 'unreal' remained unclear. Prawat *et al.* (1983) investigated the assumption that cognitive classification of objects as real or unreal depends upon the emotional attitude of the child towards them, i.e. the unreal type includes the objects which are most fearsome and terrifying. The grounds for this was the authors' belief that children get hold of their fear, driving the frightening objects away into the sphere of the unreal. The experimental data failed to confirm their hypothesis: the children (4, 7 and 10 years old), just like adults, ascribed the 'real' or 'unreal' character to 'monsters' featured in the pictures irrespective of the degree to which these monsters were regarded by them as fearsome or harmless. It also turned out that when determining the reality of the personage, preschoolers utilized the same criteria as schoolchildren and adults, mainly similarity of the objects to the objects they came across in reality.

Another important criterion for the differentiation between real and unreal objects is the belief that real objects have prototypes in the phenomenal world, whereas unreal ones exist solely as images. The possibility that the children were utilizing this criterion was investigated experimentally. Thus, Johnson and Wellman found that at the age of four children are capable of distinguishing their inner states (knowledge, memories) from real (phenomenal) external events (Johnson and Wellman, 1980). Wellman and Estes showed that even three-year-olds can tell phenomenal objects (e.g. a ball) and mental images (an imaginary ball) apart, utilizing criteria such as the presence of the phenomenal image in the perceptual field (it can be seen and touched), intersubjectivity (others can see it as well) and permanence (they have stability in time) of the phenomenal object as distinct from the similar object, presented only in imaginary form (Wellman and Estes, 1986)

At this age some children claim that the 'impossible' objects can exist just as well as mental images. A number of studies showed that as early as preschool age (4–5 years old) some children differentiate between psychic and physical phenomena, identifying mental attributes (thinking, perception, memory, etc.) with the former and physical attributes (accessibility for the sense organs, weight, motion in space, divisibility, etc.) with the latter (Johnson and Wellman, 1982; Subbotsky, 1986).

The ability of preschoolers to distinguish 'theoretically' between phenomenal and imaginary objects, ascribing 'non-existence' to the latter, contradicts the fact that these very children behave with respect to imaginary objects as if they existed in reality. This is most vividly demonstrated in their fear of an imagined object. Analysing children's fears, Staley and O'Donnell (1984) showed that among various kinds of fears, one stable specific factor was constituted by so-called night fears, with products of imagination as their objects. Typically, children's beliefs in the reality of the 'monsters' created by their own imaginations do not vanish under the influence of the information of their 'unreal character' (Jersild and Holmes, 1935).

Formulating this contradiction as a problem, Harris *et al.* (1991) undertook specific research into the existential status ascribed by children to fearsome fantastic objects: monsters, witches and ghosts. It turned out that children aged 4–6 years could tell the real phenomenal objects (a cup, a ball) from imaginary objects (an imaginary cup), which have (as in the latter case) or have not (a witch flying in the sky) a phenomenal referent; what is more, the objects of the two latter types are regarded by children as the 'unreal', non-existent objects compared with the phenomenal objects existing in reality. Despite the fact that children (particularly the six-year-olds) regarded the fantastic objects as 'fearsome', they do not ascribe to these objects a higher degree of being (reality) than to the usual imaginary objects (e.g. an imaginary pencil).

The comparison between imaginary objects of different types (the images of the real objects [e.g. 'an imaginary cup'], the images of the non-existent thought of objects ['a dog flying in the sky']) and fantastic objects ('a witch flying in the sky'), demonstrated, however, that the fantastic objects (witches and ghosts) were regarded by children as more realistic than the thought-up non-existent objects, but less realistic than the imaginary objects that have their phenomenal analogues. The authors proposed the hypothesis that children's fear of 'monsters' is based on an emotional rather than cognitive basis: although children are aware that witches and ghosts do not exist, they nevertheless emotionally 'project' them in the real world, thus ascribing them the status of really existing objects. The hypothesis was confirmed in one of the subsequent studies, in which 3–7-year-old children were found to expect an imaginary entity to appear in an empty box after they had pretended it would appear (Johnson and Harris, 1992).

On the whole, the data of the study confirmed the assumption that the children's awareness of the differences between the 'psychic' and 'physical' (i.e. imaginary-symbolic and phenomenal) is not a sufficient condition for them to develop the ability to differentiate between the spheres of reality at the level of involved behaviour (see Subbotsky, 1985).

The second trend in experimental research on the work on consciousness is the study of methods of existentialization that children of various ages employ within the sphere of everyday reality. This problem was further elaborated in studies on the ability to distinguish between *reality and appearance*.

One of the first studies to develop this trend showed that children aged five could correctly qualify visual illusions as 'appearances', if the formulation of questions contained the hint of this aspect of differentiation (Does it seem to be X? Is it really X?). If, however, the question was formulated in a neutral form, (Is it X?), the performance was much less perfect (Brain and Shanks, 1965).

Reviewing the available data Tailor and Flavell (1984) distinguished two types of error in the children's answers to the questions about appearance and reality: phenomenalistic errors (in response to the question, what is the object in reality, the children describe the phenomenal appearance of the object in the way they perceive it 'here and now') and errors of intellectual realism (in response to the request to say what the object seems to be 'here and now', the children describe the real 'known' properties of the object). A specialized study of the ability to distinguish between appearance and reality by Flavell *et al.* (1985b) demonstrated that this phenomenal type error is most common in cases when children answer questions about the features of the object (colour, shape, size), and errors of the intellectual realism type are normally made in answer to questions about identity. For example, if children are shown a red toy car and then the car is placed under a green light filter and they are asked: (1) What does the colour of the car seem to be now? (2) What is the actual colour of the car 'really and truly'? three-year-olds are more liable to answer both questions 'black' (the red car seems to be black under the green light filter). If, on the contrary, the children are shown a sponge camouflaged like a stone, encouraged to touch it and then asked the same questions (What does the object look like now: a stone or a sponge?; What is it 'really and truly'?) the children more often than not answer 'a sponge'.

Special studies in which the objects and the sequence of asking the questions varied demonstrated that the prevalence of the phenomenal answers in response to questions about features and the prevalence of the intellectual realism errors in response to questions about identity is a stable experimental fact (Tailor and Flavell, 1984). The errors in 'appearance-reality' judgements were found to be invariant with respect to certain cultural (Flavell, 1986) and semantical (Flavell *et al.*, 1985b) factors and resistant with respect to memory aids (Flavell *et al.*, 1985b).

Moreover, it turned out that three-year-old children were aware of the difference between the symbol and the object it substitutes (Flavell *et al.*, 1985a) and correctly answered questions about the original colour of the object and what it would be if the screen were taken away. It suggests that (1) children are aware that the question is about the object's colour rather than about the filter's colour; (2) they remember the original colour of the object; (3) they understand that the object will have the same colour if the filter were taken away. For all that, all these abilities turn out to be insufficient for children to solve correctly the problem 'appearance-reality'. What does the sufficient condition consist of in the author's view?

It consists in overcoming the limited character of small children's metacognitive notions, in the acquisition of the idea that one and the same object in one and the same consciousness can be simultaneously represented in different mutually contradictory forms: as the red (the basic colour) and the black (the appearant colour), as the sponge (cognized essence) and the stone (the appearant essence). For three-year-old children, however, the reality is one-dimensional: they believe that the object can be represented in consciousness only in one way. On the contrary, children aged 11–12 years and adults (college students) easily cope with problems of all types: they are able to distinguish precisely according to the 'appearance-reality' criterion, for instance, they distinguish or classify into specific subclasses realistic-looking forged objects ('good fakes'), unrealistic-looking forged objects ('poor fakes'), realistic-looking real objects and even real objects looking like forgeries. It was also assumed that the ability to distinguish between apparent and real can be related to the ability to solve conservation problems, to visual perspective taking ability and to the ability to distinguish between real and apparent emotions. Some of these hypotheses have gained experimental confirmation (Russell and Mitchell, 1985; Flavell, 1986).

While positively evaluating these studies, I should point out that they comprehend just one aspect of existentialization: the attribution of being to various types of phenomenal images and rational constructions *at the level of the uninvolved (verbal) action*. In fact, the typical tasks on the appearance-reality distinction include two different types of problems: problems based on the comparison between two phenomena (or the problem of quality) and problems based on the comparison between phenomena and rational constructions (the problem of identity).

In fact, when children are acquainted with a certain quality of the object (e.g. the colour or the size) and formulate it as the principal (or the stable) quality, they develop an initial or *basic phenomenon* of the object (e.g. the conviction that the car is red). The changes the basic phenomenon is subjected to afterwards (the car is covered with the light filter, a pencil is put into the water at a certain angle, etc.) engender the secondary or *derivative phenomenon*. The question of what the object seems to be and what it actually is 'really and truly' in respect to this or that quality is, in fact, the question of the attribution of the strong or weak statuses of being to one of these phenomena. If we assume that at a certain age a stronger status of being is ascribeed a priori to the actual phenomenon than to the potential or the past, it is quite natural to expect three-year-old children more often than not to give answers of the phenomenal type, i.e. in answer to the question, What is the object in actual fact? they enumerate the properties of the object they see at the moment (black, small). In this way they easily ascribe the higher status of being to the *derivative yet actual phenomenon* and the lesser to the *basic phenomenon* which at the moment exists only in the form of the image in memory. It is the struggle for the status between the basic and the derivative phenomenon that determines the originality of the answers of the three-year-olds in the experiments. This also makes up for the fact that if a fragment of the basic phenomenon remains within the field of actual perception (e.g. the object is not completely covered with the light filter), then it immediately overcomes the derivative phenomenon in the 'status competition'; on the other hand, all the other methods of strengthening the status of the basic phenomenon failed (Flavell *et al.*, 1985b).

In this aspect, the development of the existentialization with age is the development of the ability to 'allow for the status', i.e. to ascribe the status of being to the image of memory higher than the status of a phenomenon children are witnessing at the moment (which is unnatural, after all) by taking into account the transformations which had occurred to the original basic phenomenon (placing under the light filter, putting into the water).

A different process of existentialization takes place when children are asked about the identity (i.e. the essence) of the object. It is widely known that features (colour, size, shape) do not belong to the object's essence. A car, for instance, according to its essence, is 'an artificially produced object for the transportation of loads'; its colour as well as its size or shape are quite irrelevant here. Therefore, when the experimenter asks a question about what kind of object it seems to be, the question *is meant* to be about the qualities (i.e. about the glitter that a stone but no sponge can produce), but, in actual fact, *it is* about the essence (or about the rational construction) of the object. By this the 'seeming' appearance and 'cognized' essence of the object are counterposed. If we recall now that a rational construction when it first appears in children's minds is by its very nature ascribed a higher status of existence (because it is stable) in comparison to features (that are unstable), we can anticipate that children will answer the question by pointing out the essence rather than the visible quality. Thus, if children are shown a set consisting of a bigger and smaller object, with the smaller object being completely covered by the bigger one at the next moment, the child will reply to the question 'What does the set seem to be?' with the answer that it is 'a two-piece set', thus assigning a greater existential status to the rational construction as compared with the actually visible phenomenon. The latter is actually devoid of being, even the weak one, since it is not even mentioned in the children's answers. These are the answers interpreted as the answers of 'intellectual realism'.

Viewing the data like this prompts me to come to a slightly different interpretation of what is going on during the development of the ability to make 'appearance–reality' distinctions. Instead of being viewed as the development of *understanding* (what links the development to the particular mental function – thinking) it may be considered as the development of hierarchization of existing subjective structures along the 'scale of reality' (i.e. as the development of consciousness). Therefore, it is not the lack of *understanding* that accounts for the 'phenomenal type errors' (after all, the children do *know* what colour the object was and will be before and after the covering) but the lack of appropriate *existentialization* that leads to either domination of 'actual appearance' over basic qualities, or to domination of a rational construction over appearance. In the answers of the older children and adults the space is give to both 'weak' and 'strong' elements, so that the qualities absent in the perceptual field and appearance as opposed to essence are now considered to be 'worth mentioning'. Nevertheless, this development does not prove that older children, even acknowledging the basic qualities as 'more real' than the 'actual appearances', will use these 'verbal priorities' in their practical actions; in their practical actions they still may rely upon 'appearance' rather than upon 'elusive realities'.

Other limitations, typical of studies in this area, are that existentialization was studied only within the domain of everyday reality and only with respect to 'secondary' qualities which rest upon the fundamental structures of mind. Indeed, for the experiments on 'appearance–reality' or conservation of qualities to be even possible, children already have to have beliefs in object permanence or physical causality. In what way children attribute the fundamental structures to entities in their world within various realities of being is, therefore, the question to be examined.

Aims of the research

The work of Piaget seems to be the only detailed and comprehensive study of the development of individual consciousness. Although many of its elements have been subjected to experimental criticism, the whole of the Piagetian vision is still untouched. His picture of the structure of consciousness corresponds completely to a rationalistic view.

The main conclusions of this view are:

1. The consciousness of the newborn child is not differentiated according to spheres, levels and forms of presentation of the outer world and is, basically, dependent reality.
2. The sphere of everyday reality gradually emerges at the level of practical actions with sensorimotor objects by the end of the second year (after 18 months). Up to this time, the assimilation by the child of the phenomenal world is mainly subordinated to the laws of unusual reality of consciousness: the possibility of direct effect of subjectivity upon external objects (magical causality), the accessibility of alien subjectivity, nonpermanence of the object, permeability of solid bodies for other solid bodies, reversibility of time. After two years of age and in the course of further development, practical assimilation of the phenomenal world occurs mainly on the basis of the fundamental structures, inherent in everyday reality: object permanence, physical causality, objective space and time.

3. At the first stages of development of *verbal behaviour** (2–4 years old), the child assimilates the world basing itself again on the fundamental structures of unusual reality (in his or her symbolic play, dreams, reasoning). By the age of 11–12, verbal behaviour is also subordinate to the norms inherent in the fundamental structures of everyday reality. By that time unusual reality gradually leaves the centre of the individual consciousness and loses its formerly 'strong' status of being.

4. In the sphere of everyday reality, complete (or 'strong') being is assigned to rational constructions. With the emergence of rational constructions in the child's consciousness (as elementary logic, physical, mathematical, etc. notions) the phenomena which do not correspond to their relevant rational constructions lose the status of complete being and cease to regulate the practical behaviour of the child.

5. A contemporary adult in a state of normal alertness and acting in full conscience, assimilates the phenomenal world basing him or herself almost exclusively upon the fundamental structures of everyday reality.

This theoretical analysis of the structure of individual consciousness encourages me to subject Piaget's schema to a critical reassessment. First of all, this reassessment is prompted by:

1. The 'linear' character or representation of the development of consciousness, according to which consciousness is initially constructed on the basis of unusual fundamental structures and afterwards almost wholly based on everyday structures (the 'replacement' model).

2. The reduction of the study of the realities of consciousness in children older than four years to the studies of verbal behaviour under the implicit assumption that real behaviour at this age is totally subordinated to the fundamental structures of everyday reality.

3. The drawing of a rigid border between everyday and unusual realities: the assimilation of sensorimotor objects by preschool-age children and

---

* For ease in describing experimental studies, the terms 'verbal' and 'real' behaviour will stand for the terms 'uninvolved' and 'involved' levels of behaviour, although in principle there is no necessary correspondence between the former and the latter.

adults both on the levels of practical actions and verbal judgements within everyday reality cannot occur on the basis of the fundamental structures of unusual reality.

4. The assumption of the de-existentialization of the phenomenal layer of consciousness: with the adoption by the child of rational constructions, phenomena gradually cease to regulate the child's behaviour.

Alternative hypotheses can be formulated as follows:

1. Individual consciousness, at both levels of behaviour and throughout the whole life-span, is, in fact, a heterogeneous, pluralistic integrity incorporating both the elements of everyday and unusual realities.

2. The development of individual consciousness does not occur in the form of a linear stage-by-stage substitution of one domain of reality for another; rather, it is an increasing differentiation between the domains of realities with their subsequent coexistence (the 'coexistence' model).

3. The spheres of reality are not dependent upon the levels of behaviour, due to which the child and an adult can, for instance, practically assimilate the sensorimotor objects basing themselves on unusual fundamental structures, whereas at the level of verbal judgements they still rest on the norms of everyday reality.

4. With the development of symbolic rational constructions the phenomenal layer of consciousness does not necessarily lose its significance, and in certain conditions continues to regulate the real behaviour of an individual competing in this role with rational constructions.

My examination of these hypotheses consists of research into the peculiarities of the fundamental structures of consciousness at the various stages of ontogenesis.

Chapter 2

The development of the stable object concept in ontogenesis

The concept of the stable object underlies early concepts of space, time and causality and constitutes the foundation for individual consciousness. In order to interact meaningfully with another person or object, a subject must be convinced of their continued existence even during their physical absence. It is due to our belief in object permanence that our universe consists of steady objects and continual chains of events, whereas magic and witchcraft are exiled to the domain of dreams and fairy tales. Development of the object concept is also related to subsequent cognitive development, for example, in the acquisition of relational words (Wachs, 1975; Tomasello and Farrar, 1984, 1986).

Research in the object concept development was pioneered by Piaget (1936, 1937), who described its development over the course of six stages. In the first two stages (0–3 months), the concept exists only as a primitive associative-emotional schema. In the third stage (approximately 3–7 months), some prerequisites of object permanence appear. But the infant's belief in the object's permanence exists solely as a function of activity with the object. At stage 4 (approximately 8–12 months), infants can retrieve a hidden object. However, if an object that was initially hidden and retrieved at point A is transferred to point B and again occluded, the infant will continue to search at A (the AB error). At stage 5 (approximately 12–17 months) identification of an object with its initial location disappears. The infant now searches for an object where it was last, not first, hidden, but only so long as the move to point B takes place in plain view. Finally, at stage 6 (from 18 months), the child has no problem with hidden transpositions. Even if the object is hidden, it is 'conserved' in representational form.

Thus, according to Piaget, children learn to attribute existence to objects by interacting with them on a sensorimotor level during the first two years of life. A central parameter in successful existence attribution is object permanence – a rule that an object continues to exist even after it disappears from the perceptual field. This 'permanence rule' (PR) is fully functional in two-year-old children whereas younger infants tend to make use of the opposite 'discontinuity rule' (DR). They lack object permanence and assume discontinuity of existence when the object is removed from their immediate perceptual field. In other words the permanence rule presupposes that (1) the object cannot become non-existent once its existence has been established; (2) the object cannot spontaneously change into a completely different one; and (3) the object cannot be destroyed or reconstructed by pure mental effort of the subject without the use of any material tools and actions.

In more recent years the phenomenon has been studied in great depth by a number of researchers. Some of these studies set out to confirm the validity of Piaget's assumed stages (Gratch and Landers, 1971; Gouin-Décarie, 1974). Others aimed to achieve more sophisticated experimental verification of the parameters involved in successful application of the permanence rule (Butterworth, 1975; Cossete-Ricard, 1983; Freeman, Lloyd and Sinha, 1980; Harris, 1973; LeCompte and Gratch, 1972; Lucas and Uzgiris, 1977; Schuberth, Werner and Lipsitt, 1978; Webb, Massar and Nadolny, 1972). In a third approach, there has been an attempt to generalize the experimental data in terms of computer models in the development of object permanence (Luger, Bower and Wishart, 1983; Luger, Wishart and Bower, 1984; Prazdny, 1980).

Bower (1971), in a series of ingenious experiments, demonstrated that children as young as five months have object permanence. Other researchers, however, have reinterpreted many of Bower's findings in terms of reactions to learnt event sequences rather than true demonstrations of object permanence in very young infants (Haith and Campos, 1977; Harris, 1975).

In the studies by Baillargeon (Baillargeon, 1987; Baillargeon *et al.*, 1985) infants as young as 3½ months were shown to believe that objects continue to exist even when occluded and are impermeable to another solid object. Le Compte and Gratch (1972) showed that infants repeatedly found an object hidden in a box. The object was then placed in the box and, when uncovered, proved to be a different object. Both nine- and eighteen-month-olds were surprised by this occurrence, but only

eighteen-month-old infants searched for the original object. Similar results were obtained by Ramsay and Campos (1975, 1978). These data
support the view that active representation does not appear until stage 6.

The development of object permanence in childhood

Although Piaget suggested that in the domain of verbal intelligence the
development of a stable object concept is not completed until the age of
11 or 12 years (Piaget, 1937a, b), he and most researchers generally
assumed that in the sensorimotor domain the parameters that constitute
object stability for the two-year-old remain constant throughout the life-
span. This assumption being taken for granted, it obviates the need for
further study of object permanence, at least with respect to sensorimotor
objects. However, certain data show that under special circumstances
children older than two believe that permanence rules can be violated in
real life; as a result, nonpermanent, imaginary objects may acquire the
'real' status of physical objects (Harris *et al.*, 1991).

These data contradict the view that a child ascribes only impermanence
to all objects in the first months of life, but by the age of two has developed
a capacity for representation and attribution of permanence to physical
objects. Thereafter this capacity totally dominates in the sensorimotor
sphere. To me, this viewpoint seems incorrect for two reasons. First, the
properties impermanence and permanence are categorical opposites and
can enter consciousness (even at the level of the prereflexive sensorimotor
intelligence) only *simultaneously*. Second, the child's rejection, on the basis
of his or her own experience, of either of these orientations (e.g. impermanence) considered in isolation is theoretically impossible since the very
realizability of 'experience' is necessarily based on the existence of both of
these orientations. For example, empirical confirmation that an object that
has disappeared behind a screen has not disappeared from the world already presupposes that the child has an idea of permanence in his or her
consciousness. This means that the search for forms of behaviour indicating the existence of both a rule of permanence and a rule of impermanence
in a child of any age is theoretically justified.

I assume that what happens in children's consciousness as they grow
older and acquire experience is not a replacement of some fundamental

structures by others (a rule of impermanence for a rule of permanence), but rather a differentiation of its spheres. In the different spheres of individual consciousness, the assimilation or interpretation of the same phenomenon takes place through different fundamental structures. For instance, permanence rules may dominate in the domain of everyday reality, whereas nonpermanence rules may dominate in the domain of the unusual, such as dreams, fairy tales and fantasy play. Under some conditions, however, nonpermanence rules may transcend the boundaries separating the two domains.

The test of the hypotheses presented required an experimental design in which the child would encounter violation of the permanence of existence of an object and would be forced to explain and assimilate this.

To this end, we used a wooden box $15 \times 11 \times 11$ cm firmly covered with a lid (see Subbotsky, 1990). The bottom of the box was covered with black velvet. When the lid was closed, a metallic plate (also covered with velvet) separated from the inside of the front wall and noiselessly slid to the bottom, completely covering it. When the lid was lifted again, it was impossible to notice any changes, since the system of magnets in the wall of the box and at its bottom ensured that it was impossible to discover a double bottom no matter how the box was manipulated (see Figure 2.1). This simple setup enabled us to carry out all three possible variants of violation of permanence: *transformation* (e.g. a piece of paper was in the box, but a postage stamp later appeared), *disappearance* (the postage stamp was initially there, but then it disappeared), and *generation* (the box was empty, but later the postage stamp appeared). The phenomenon of impermanence appeared because the object changed its features despite the fact that two other parameters (spatiotemporal continuity and the mode of disappearance) remained unchanged and characteristic of a permanent object. In other words, it was impossible to explain the transformation of the piece of paper into a postage stamp by saying that the 'paper had been taken out, and the postage stamp put in' (violation of spatiotemporal continuity) or by saying that 'the paper dissolved, evaporated, etc.' (violation of the requirement 'method of disappearance guaranteeing the permanence of the object'). Throughout the entire experiment, the experimenter did not touch the box and was 2–2.5 metres from it.

The additional objects used were: a small piece of paper with a telephone number written on it by pen, a big postage stamp, a cardboard box with a lid ($5 \times 5 \times 10$ cm), a silver ring with a stone, a cigarette lighter, etc.

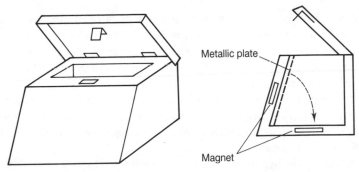

Figure 2.1 The wooden box in front view and in cross-section

In this study, children of 4–6 years of age observed all the above-mentioned instances of nonpermanence: (1) the sudden disappearance of a physical object, (2) one object inexplicably turning into another, and (3) a new object created 'from nothing'.

Thus one of the conditions focused on the disappearance of an object. At the preliminary session the child was called into the experimental room. There was a cardboard box on the table, and a piece of paper and a postage stamp were lying there with it. The experimenter asked the child the following questions:

1. If I place a piece of paper in this cardboard box, can this red postage stamp show up there in place of the paper or not? Why? Can this happen in a fairy tale?
2. Can this happen: I take an empty box, I close it, I open it up, and there is a postage stamp in it. Why? Can this happen in a fairy tale?
3. Could the following occur: I place a postage stamp in the empty box, close it, open it up again, and the box is empty, there is nothing in it. Why? Can this happen in a fairy tale?

Then the child was told the story of the 'Magic box', the gist of which was briefly as follows: An acquaintance comes to visit the parents of a little girl, Masha. When he leaves, he gives her a wooden box that can transform simple pieces of paper into pretty postage stamps (a picture of the box is shown). At first Masha does not believe it, but after she tests it, she becomes convinced of the magic properties of the box. After the subject was able to repeat the content of the story satisfactorily, he or she was asked the following questions: 'Why did the piece of paper become a postage stamp for Masha?' 'Does this mean that such a thing can happen?' 'Really, or only in a fairy tale?'

The purpose of the first session of the experiment was to determine: (1) whether the child admitted the possibility of violation of the permanence of the existence of an object (transformation, disappearance, generation) in everyday and fairy-tale reality; (2) whether encountering an instance of violation of permanence (in the fairy tale) had any influence on the child's belief that such a thing could not happen 'in reality'. Thus, we attempted to determine whether differentiation of the rule of permanence and the rule of impermance took place between the spheres of reality at the level of verbal behaviour, and how stable this differentiation was.

At a second session the child was again called into the room in which the same box was located. The experimenter assured the child that the box had a magic property: if one placed a postage stamp in it, it would become a ring, a cigarette lighter, or a necklace – 'whichever you want' (the objects are shown). Then the experimenter went out of the room and for five minutes observed the child's behaviour. If the child put the previously obtained postage stamp in the box and closed it, when he or she opened it again the box would be empty. When the experimenter returned, the following interview was conducted: 'Well, did you try?' 'Did you succeed?' 'But where's the postage stamp?' 'Did it completely disappear, or simply go away somewhere?' 'If you search well, will you find it or not?' 'Why did the postage stamp disappear?'

The purpose of the second session was to determine whether the child would turn to a magic action (closing and opening the box plus appropriate manipulations with the paper or the postage stamp) in the sphere of everyday reality for the purpose of obtaining the desired object (the postage stamp, the ring, etc.). Actually, if the child treated the object (piece of paper, postage stamp) as permanent, implementation of the magic manipulations as described in the fairy tale would have no meaning, and the box would be assimilated by purely rational devices (examination, search for a mechanism, etc.). But if the child resorted to specific magical manipulations, this meant that he or she was counting on a transformation (generation) and consequently ascribed the property of impermanence to the object.

However, such an interpretation of the child's behaviour requires refinement: To what extent can magical manipulations be considered magical actions, not simply 'let's pretend' actions? In other words, it is necessary to demonstrate that in carrying out magical manipulations, the child really is counting on a transformation, is not simply playing 'magic box'. Moreover, even if a child, in carrying out a magical manipulation really does count on 'making a postage stamp out of a piece of paper', it is still necessary to prove that he or she has actually carried out a 'magical transformation' and is not simply 'printing' the stamp on paper by means of a special 'machine'. For technical solution of this problem it might be helpful to distinguish between productive actions and search actions. *Productive actions* are actions whose purpose is to produce a material object existing at a given moment only as a representation in the mind. *Search* actions are actions whose purpose is to discover an object existing both as a part of the imagination and as a material object, but not present in the field of perception at the particular moment. Productive actions can in turn be subdivided into (1) rational productive actions: the person creates an object, depicting clearly all stages of its genesis from the appropriate initial materials (cutting out little flags from paper); (2) phenomenal productive actions: a person creates an object, carrying out only some 'starting' actions and not knowing the 'intermediate' mechanism for producing the object (e.g. putting coins in a vending machine with soda water); (3) magical productive actions: a person creates an object or influences the course of events by the direct 'materialization of a wish', a magical act, or a 'magic word' (e.g. 'knock on wood', 'spit over your shoulder', etc.).

Actions of types (1) and (2) are based on the norm of permanence and are always aimed at some sensory objects (material, instrument, etc.) from which the target object is produced, or at some apparatus in which the target is actually or potentially already contained.

Actions of type (3) are based on the norm of impermanence and are directed towards producing an object that is not in a state of material being, i.e. creation of an object 'out of nothing, toward the materialization of a thought'. Hence, it is clear that though actions of types (2) and (3) are externally similar, their psychological contents are fundamentally different; empirically, this difference derives from the fact that if an action of type (2) is ineffective (the coin is inserted in the machine, but no soda water comes out), the action has a tendency to become a *search action* (beating with one's fists on the machine, seeking out a mechanic, etc.), whereas frustration of an action of type (3) does not provoke search behaviour, but merely results in repetition of a magical ritual over and over again.

Thus, if a child's magical manipulations with the box were of a play nature (and the child was therefore not counting on a transformation or a genesis), then, having encountered the phenomenon in all three subseries of experiments, he or she should seek the disappeared object (or the place from whence the postage stamp had appeared). On the other hand, if the actions were of a productive magical nature, then search behaviour should not be observed in any of the subseries, but only multiple repetitions of attempts to exert a magical influence (i.e. magical manipulations). The first variant of behaviour signifies that the child has assimilated the phenomenon, relying on the norm of permanence, whereas the second indicates that the child's actual behaviour is based on the norm of impermanence. Finally, if the child has engaged in no search in situations of 'transformation' and 'generation', but has displayed search behaviour in a situation of 'disappearance', then in the first two situations the action has been based on the norm of impermanence, whereas in the latter situation, it has been based on the norm of permanence and is a productive-phenomenal act (i.e. it led to search only in the case of failure).

The second objective index of the child's use of the norm of permanence or of impermanence was emotional experience, outwardly expressed in facial expression, pantomime and vocal reactions. We thought that the emotion of surprise in a particular situation would indicate that the child was experiencing a state of discrepancy between an expected and the actually occurring event, and that the degree of surprise would be proportional to the degree of discrepancy. In this study two types of discrepancy were possible: (1) a discrepancy between the norm that was ascribed to the existence of the object (rule of permanence) and the 'behaviour' of the object itself (impermanence); (2) a discrepancy between the expectation that some pragmatic need would be satisfied (obtaining a postage stamp or a ring) and the actual event leading to the nonsatisfaction of this need.

Hence, it follows that if the child's actions were based on the norm of permanence (e.g. if they were play actions) then, first, the phenomenon should produce surprise in all three subseries; second, the degree of surprise in a situation of 'disappearance' should be greater than in the other two, since a discrepancy of both types occurred only in this situation. But if the child's actions were based on the norm of impermanence, no signs of surprise upon observing the phenomena of 'transformation' and 'generation' should be observed.

The experiment with a control group was conducted in another kindergarten and included only the 'disappearance' situation.

The children were called into the room on the pretext of 'studying their ability to name objects'. They were promised a pretty postage stamp if they did well. As the fake assignment was performed (naming objects in a picture), the children were asked to place a postage stamp in an empty box standing beside it and to close the box; after the work was finished, they were told to take the postage stamp out of the box and go back to their group. At this moment the experimenter went out of the room and observed the children's behaviour for five minutes through a screen; but the children, opening the box, found that it was empty. When the experimenter returned to the room, he conducted an interview similar to that described in the preceding series.

Preliminary questioning revealed that almost all of the subjects believed in the possibility of spontaneous change, appearance and disappearance of material objects in a fairy tale setting, but denied that these phenomena could occur in everyday reality. They reported disbelief in the possibility that the box could destroy or create material objects.

In spite of this, in the experimental situation most of the children behaved as if magical disappearance or creation took place in everyday life. Thus, if a postage stamp suddenly disappeared from the box resulting in a loss of reward neither surprise nor search behaviour could be observed in the participating children. Instead, they continually repeated the 'magical' act of opening and closing the lid. This seems to indicate that a child's behaviour continues to be regulated by the discontinuity rule under some circumstances, even when the object is perfectly open to sensorimotor manipulation as is the case with the postage stamp and a piece of paper. In contrast, children in the control condition were extremely surprised by the disappearance and searched for the object that had disappeared (Figure 2.2).

In the third session (the postexperiment interview) in the 'Transformation' situation, not one child drew on the norm of permanence, whereas in the 'Generation' situation, only children in the preparatory group did so. In the 'Disappearance' situation, subjects in all groups drew on the norm of permanence – moreover, much more frequently than in the 'Generation' situation. Thus, *it was much easier for a child to acknowledge the impermanence of an object when it arose from some other object than when the object arose from nothing or was transformed into nothing.*

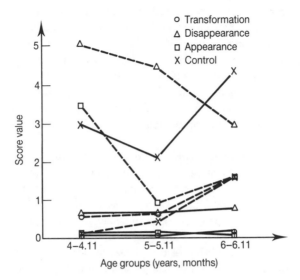

Figure 2.2 Average values for the indices of search actions (——) and magical manipulations (– – –) in conditions

Basically, the data show that assimilation of the same phenomenon (for example, 'Disappearance') at the level of verbal and actual behaviour, respectively, can rely on different norms of attribution of existence (the norm of impermanence and the norm of permanence), and that the unity of verbal and actual behaviour increases somewhat in older children. Furthermore, it was found that: (1) observation of the phenomenon of apparent impermanence altered, in an essential way, the strategy of verbal behaviour of most of the children in the experimental groups, from the norm of permanence to that of impermanence; (2) the children were most reluctant to use the impermanence rule in the situation in which the use of the norm of impermanence was not advantageous for the child (thus, the number of search actions in the 'disappearance' condition was significantly higher than in the other two experimental conditions); (3) there was a disproportionality between verbal and actual behaviour in subjects of the experimental groups.

As studies have shown (Le Compte and Gratch, 1972), from the age of nine months a child begins to display external signs of *surprise* when an object that, before his or her eyes, is placed in a container and covered with a screen is replaced; and at the age of 18 months, he or she begins actively to search for the disappeared object. Other investigators date the appearance of search behaviour in such a situation even earlier, e.g. 8–10 months (Ramsay and Campos, 1975, 1978). When a moving object that passes behind a screen is replaced, children have shown surprise after reaching the age of 16 months (Gratch, 1982). Following Piaget, investigators have interpreted these findings as a sign of a transition from the capacity for passive identification of previously seen objects to their active representation and, consequently, ascription to them of permanence of existence.

In light of our findings, this picture of the genesis of a child's conceptions of a stable object stands in need of major correction. First, the emergence of the capacity for representation of an object in the sixth stage of sensorimotor development is a necessary but not sufficient condition for attributing the property of permanence to the object. A representative image of an object is only one of the forms of its existence in consciousness; but attribution of the properties of full existence to this image (i.e. the property of symbolizing some real material object existing in reality, but at the particular moment not in the field of perception) is a very special process, conditioned by the *normative structure* of consciousness that has developed in a specific cultural-historical situation. In other words, whether a child beyond the age of two will or will not ascribe complete existence (i.e. permanence) to an object that has left his or her field of vision will depend on a number of conditions such as: (1) in what sphere of individual consciousness this event takes place (everyday or unusual reality); (2) the specific conditions of disappearance (appearance, transformation) of the object in the sphere of everyday reality (passing behind a screen, explosion, dissolving, etc.); whether or not the parameters of identity of the object are violated in this case, and if yes, then which one; (3) at which level of consciousness the phenomenon is assimilated (actual behaviour, verbal behaviour); and (4) which of the fundamental structures (the norm of impermanence or the norm of permanence) most satisfactorily meets the subject's basic needs. Let us look at these conditions.

The present data have shown that almost all the children studied readily acknowledged the possibility of spontaneous transformation, generation and disappearance of an object within the context of a fairy tale, but denied this possibility in the sphere of everyday reality. The causes of this phenomenon are very obvious: in a fairy tale, in play and in art, which are special spheres of reality given to the child by society, impermanence is specially cultivated and, together with permanence, occupies a legitimate and even dominant position. The sudden transformation, unexpected appearance and disappearance of objects, like magical causality, are an inseparable attribute of the fairy tale; they are its very basis, and stand in contrast to 'realistic' forms of construing and representing the world. In contrast, in the sphere of everyday reality, opposing properties (permanence, physical causality) are attributed to an object while contrasting norms (impermanence, magic) are relegated to the 'background' (possible but not real). As a result, for a child of a specific age, 'experience', in the natural science sense of that word, becomes possible when, for example, the revelation of an object that has previously disappeared behind a screen is regarded as a *proof* of its permanence, not as 'regeneration' of a similar object through the accomplishment of a search ritual. Traces of the active influence of both fundamental structures (the norm of permanence and the norm of impermanence) are already evident in infancy and early childhood (Subbotsky, 1987), but the possibility of differentiation between spheres of consciousness emerges only with the appearance of symbolic means for representing and transforming the world; this possibility is the actual process of creating 'ecological niches' for the active influence of incompatible fundamental structures.

Further, it was found that at the level of verbal, 'abstract', remote discussion, the children emphatically denied the efficacy of the phenomenon of impermanence (which fully fits the hierarchy of fundamental structures ordering everyday reality); but at the level of actual behaviour, most of the subjects (experimental group) behaved as if the transformation, disappearance, and generation 'out of nothing' actually took place. In other words, at the level of discussion, the culturally given dominance of the norm of permanence emerged earlier than at the level of actual behaviour, in which the child continued to make use of the two incompatible structures. On the whole, this fits in with data indicating that verbal behaviour changes more rapidly under the influence of normative cultural processing: at this level, for example, the norms of moral behaviour, altruism, independence and the attribution of physical causality begin to function for the first time (Subbotsky, 1983, 1985). In contrast, at the level of actual behaviour, the hypothetical boundary between spheres of consciousness is more blurred and indeterminate, and the norm of impermanence penetrates the sphere of everyday reality more easily. However, this penetration takes place only under certain conditions: (1) when an event of transformation (disappearance, generation) initially takes place in the sphere of everyday reality; (2) when the adult in his or her instructions assumes the possibility of this event occurring in the sphere of everyday reality (saying that the box has been 'taken from the fairy tale'). If these conditions arc not present (i.e. if the boundary separating the spheres of reality is not artificially 'punctured'), children draw on the norm of permanence at the level of actual behaviour (in the control group). It should be especially stressed that in this particular case, the adult's instructions have only an *indirect* influence, breaking the previously evolved hierarchy of norms; and there is certainly no directive 'introduction' of the norm of impermanence. The guarantee preventing such directiveness is the absence of external control or supervision at the moment the phenomenon is assimilated at the level of actual behaviour, so that the child is able freely to choose any method of action. It may be assumed that under natural conditions, the causes of such a break in the hierarchy of norms may also be different: physical or mental exhaustion, stress, a powerful frustrated need, and other factors resulting in the emergence of 'special states of consciousness'.

Our findings indirectly testify to the influence of the emotional and need sphere on the way phenomena are assimilated: we found that in cases in which attribution of the property of impermanence to the object contributed to satisfaction of a need to obtain a reward (transformation, generation), the child more readily made use of it as an instrument for assimilating the phenomena than when attribution of the norm of impermanence resulted in nonsatisfaction of a pragmatic wish (disappearance). It is conceivable that this selective violation of the evolved hierarchy of norms and the preference for 'false' means for assimilating phenomena reveal the phenomenon of 'partisanship' familiar in psychology (Subbotsky, 1978b), whose originality in this particular case consists merely in the fact that it is not ordinary facts and methods of action that are subject to biased selection, but the most fundamental structures of consciousness.

There is one more finding worthy of attention, namely, the change in the children's verbal behaviour under the influence of observation of the phenomena. Whereas before the phenomena were observed all the children were convinced of their impossibility, afterwards many had changed their opinion and explained what had taken place by drawing on the norm of impermanence. This is one more piece of evidence of the considerable variability of verbal behaviour, its susceptibility to external influences, and its relative independence of the level of actual behaviour. Indeed, correlations of the utilization of the norm of permanence and the norm of impermanence in assimilating phenomena at different levels indicate that a considerable number of the subjects relied on opposing structures.

As in the case of the preceding phenomenon (Subbotsky, 1978), a factor of a more particular nature had a modulating influence on this general law: the children more readily admitted the norm of impermanence in their interpretation of the phenomenon of spontaneous transformation than in their interpretation of disappearance or generation from nothing. The reasons for this are not difficult to understand: despite the unusualness of the phenomenon of sudden transformation, it none the less does fit in, to a greater extent, with the experience of everyday reality, in which transformations of some particular objects into others (e.g. water into ice) take place constantly, than do phenomena in which an object disappears without a trace or appears out of nothing.

In sum, the main finding of this study is that belief in physical object nonpermanence does not belong exclusively to infancy: it may also be found among preschool age children. The question arises whether it is true with regard to adults as well.

The development of object permanence in adulthood

It might be assumed that a demonstration of object nonpermanence to adult subjects cannot produce valuable scientific results, save for the reproduction of the already known fact that adults believe in object permanence. However, I think that such a demonstration can yet bring results which might have a certain scientific value with two respects.

First, it can determine the conditions under which an educated person might nevertheless believe in object nonpermanence. The very existence of widespread religious beliefs, as well as of the so-called 'paranormal beliefs' (see, for example, Zusne and Jones, 1982) testify in favour of this possibility.

Second, a demonstration of physical object nonpermanence might provide the possibility of determining psychological mechanisms which are brought to work in order to conserve the person's belief in object permanence. In other words, it can help to answer the question: What psychological processes are involved in the case when a person who believes strongly in object permanence has to explain the nonpermanence of a physical object, if he or she observes the nonpermanence? It is possible that under these conditions certain violations of the normal work of psychological functions (such as memory, perception, logical thinking) could take place. If the problem is put like that, the novelty of the expected results might presumably be in determining what subjects are prepared to sacrifice in order to keep their belief in object permanence.

In comparison with research on the development of object permanence in infancy, surprisingly few researchers have investigated the parameters that determine acknowledgement of existence of objects and object permanence in adults. One notable exception is Michotte, who conducted a number of important studies. Michotte (1962) reported that a subject was inclined to judge an object 'the same', i.e. identical to one seen previously, if only one of four features, form, dimension, colour or spatial location, had been changed. If, however, two or more characteristics had been changed simultaneously, subjects tended to report that they believed that one object had been replaced with another. In other words, for adults an object's identity is determined not by its separate qualities but by the overall combination of these qualities (the object's Gestalt). Michotte's contribution resulted in a careful analysis of the perceptual conditions under which adults ascribed permanence to phenomenal objects.

Warren (1977) showed that an object which moved and changed its shape simultaneously was perceived as the same only if there was some sensible explanation for the change. For example, when presented with an object that alternately took the shape of a square and a trapezoid, subjects were able to interpret this as a door which was opening and closing. In cases that were devoid of such an explanation an alternation of two different objects was perceived.

Although these studies are very interesting, the ensuing results are nevertheless entirely phenomenological in nature and do not answer the question of whether adult subjects would, in certain circumstances, ascribe discontinuity to material objects in real life. The purpose of the present study, therefore, was to answer the central and fundamental question, whether adults, under some conditions, use the discontinuity rule in situations concerning everyday material objects.

Seventy-five subjects took part in the experiment ranging in age from 17 to 43 with a mean age of 26.2. Most of the subjects were professionals, all educated to university degree level, although some first-year psychology students at Moscow University also took part. All the subjects were native Russian speakers. The experiment was conducted in Moscow in 1987.

The box described earlier in this Chapter (Figure 2.1) was employed in the experiment.

Subjects were told that the aim of the study was to investigate their judgements with respect to the existence of material objects. The experimenter pointed to the postage stamp, which was lying clearly visible on the table close to the box, and asked the first set of core questions: What is that? Does the postage stamp exist? Why do you think that? The purpose of these questions was to examine the reasoning behind subjects' attribution of existence to a stable material object in their perceptual fields.

The subject was then asked to put the postage stamp into the box and close the lid. A further set of core questions followed: Does that postage stamp still exist? Why do you think that? But you cannot see or touch it; why do you think it still exists? The purpose of these questions was to establish what reasoning determined existence attribution to objects that had been removed from the perceptual field. In the three experimental conditions subjects next observed the experimenter's attempt 'to influence the postage stamp by willpower'. The experimenter brought his hands close to the box from both sides to a distance of about 10 to 15 cm. Looking intently at the box he seemed to exert great effort, an impression conveyed by means of a strained face, trembling hands and an expression of concentration. After a few seconds he removed his hands and asked the third set of core questions: Do you believe that this postage stamp disappeared from the face of this earth or has turned into another postage stamp? Please tell me the probability with which you believe this?

Probability estimates had to be produced on a 0–100 per cent scale. A probability of 0 per cent meant absolute certainly that the event did not occur, 100 per cent probability was taken to represent complete certainty that the event did occur, and 50 per cent probability indicated that the subject believed in both possibilities to an equal extent. The purpose of these questions was to establish whether subjects were prepared to admit to the possibility of mental transformation or disappearance of a material object without any physical contact. The subject was then instructed to remove the stamp from the box and to put it on the table. Opening the box the subject found one of three possible 'transformed' objects, which had been hidden between the metal plate and the wall of the box prior to the commencement of the experiment. Either a previously torn and crumpled stamp had become new (reconstruction), or a new stamp had become torn and old (destruction), or the postage stamp had changed from a small one to a bigger, entirely different one (transformation).

In the course of the ensuing conversation the experimenter put a further set of core questions to the subject: What is this? Is this the same object that you put into the box or is it another object? Do you notice any change in the object? Did you notice the change at once or only after my last question? The experimenter then attempted to extract a spontaneous explanation of what had happened from the subject.

It was assumed that subjects handling the phenomenon with reference to the permanence rule would have to argue as follows. First, they would have to insist that there was a new object, while second, acknowledging the continued existence of the old object somewhere else. This should lead to the conclusion that the latter had been somehow substituted by the former. If, on the other hand, subjects considered the new and the original stamp to be identical, they would be required to explain the fact of transformation without physical influence. In order to preserve the permanence rule, subjects had to find an explanation in terms of natural causes or, alternatively, accept that the object had been transformed by mental effort thus adopting the discontinuity rule. In order to obtain quantifiable results subjects were asked to produce further probability estimates for three alternative hypotheses about what had happened. These were presented by the experimenter as follows:

1. I have the ability to change (destroy, renew or turn into another) small material objects without touching them, by means of pure willpower only.
2. I hypnotized you and exchanged the postage stamps while you were asleep. I also induced post-hypnotic amnesia so that you cannot remember anything that happened to you.
3. It was just a trick.

Towards the end of the experiment subjects were invited to estimate the probability of existence of a number of unexplained or mysterious phenomena, using the same scale as before. These included the possibility that 'unidentified flying objects' might be cosmic stations of civilizations from outer space, the existence of genuine parapsychological phenomena, the actual existence of the 'abominable snowman' and the Loch Ness monster, as well as the possibilities that there is some omnipotent intelligence that created the universe and is the cause of its laws, and that the human soul continues to exist beyond death. The aim here was to assess the probability of existence an individual subject was prepared to attribute to unusual and enigmatic phenomena in order to examine any relationship between this kind of belief and belief in mental transformation of material objects.

The general idea was, first, to get a clear picture of what type of beliefs and superstitions European adults hold, and second, to establish whether the observation of an unusual phenomenon, the apparent discontinuity of a material object, can influence the magnitude of such beliefs.

Our data (see Figs 2.3 and 2.4 (pp. 65 and 67) for Russian subjects) demonstrate that adults do ascribe permanence to stable material objects and believe that objects remain identical even when removed from their perceptual fields, i.e. positioned behind a screen, provided that the object, albeit behind a screen, is permanently under visual and attentional control. Observing the experimenter's efforts to influence the object by 'willpower' does not have any effect on subjects' opinions on this matter. Mean subjective probability with regard to the mental effort hypothesis was low and non-significant. In attributing permanence to the object, subjects usually appealed to the apparent lack of violation of the following 'identity parameters'. First, the object disappeared from the visual field in a manner that precluded any change in the object's structure; second, there was spatiotemporal continuity of observation of the events; and third, the absence of any external intervention.

In fact, subjects reported that the object disappeared in such a way that it was neither destroyed nor changed ('I put it into the box myself, nothing happened to it'), that the object was constantly present under the continuous control of the subject ('I have been watching the box all the time, there could not have been any substitution'), and that the object was not subject to any external forces ('You did not touch it, so it cannot have changed').

To this point the results strongly support the notion of a modern person as rationalist and materialist, ascribing permanence to a material object in at least two of the three experimental situations, i.e. presence and absence of the object from the visual field. Nevertheless, when the subjects opened the box the object proved to have changed, that is, an *impossible event* had taken place. This is a crucial problem in the present research which aims to determine whether or not a modern educated person is prepared to accept the possibility of object discontinuity in everyday reality. Theoretically, there are three possible ways of resolving this problem. Subjects could either deny the fact that the object has changed, or they could admit that one of the identity parameters must have been violated in some way, or they could acknowledge that an 'impossible event' had taken place. All the three cases were observed in this experiment. First, it was found that a substantial number of subjects did not notice the substitution. This can be interpreted as the denial of an impossible event on the level of a subconscious perceptive mechanism. It is interesting to note that denial took place only in the two reconstruction conditions and not in the destruction condition, although all three employed exactly the same stimuli (new and old identical stamps). Second, finding themselves unable to retrieve the original object subjects began to express doubt about the integrity of the identity parameters. Some of them forwarded explanations that presumed destruction of the original object due to, for instance, a chemical process or the presence of some hidden mechanism. Others thought that spatiotemporal continuity of their conscious presence (or at least their attention) had been violated in some way, possibly by means of hypnosis or distraction of their attention on behalf of the experimenter. Logical identification of original and new objects was significantly stronger in the destruction condition than in the transformation or reconstruction conditions. Presumably, this fact can be explained by reference to the 'law of entropy'. According to this, it is easier to create a destructive hidden mechanism (chemical or mechanical) than one that is capable of creation (reproduction of a new object given an old and broken one).

Third and last, the most interesting variant in terms of this research was subjects' acknowledgement of the possibility of 'mental transformation' of a postage stamp. This yields the violation of one of the most generally applicable rules of rational existence attribution: The existence of a material object does not depend on the subject's thoughts, will, or desires. This type of explanation for the phenomenon is at variance with the foundations of modern *scientific* thinking, and that is why it is forwarded only *under specific conditions*.

First of all, the results of the control reconstruction condition show that the subjects do not arrive at this hypothesis spontaneously. When the experimenter provides cues, such as in the three experimental conditions, subjects are not prepared to concede this possibility either. Even if the transforming condition was observed, subjects very rarely expressed the idea that it was 'mental effort' that had changed the object, but rather preferred the other two kinds of explanation. Only direct proposal of this 'impossible' idea by the experimenter led a majority of the subjects to adopt this hypothesis as a serious option. Altogether 64 per cent of subjects attributed an MSP greater than nil to this option. The results closely match those found with preschool children: they only used the discontinuity rule during the experiment, if they had received instructions from the experimenter confirming the possibility of discontinuity (Subbotsky, 1990a).

The fact remains that subjects are more prone to acknowledge 'mental effort' as a factor in the destruction condition than under either the reconstruction or the transformation conditions. Again one is tempted to interpret this as a belief in the law of entropy, that destructive forces (here purely mental ones) are easier to invoke than constructive ones. In the destruction condition subjects are least inclined to explain the phenomenon by reference to 'hypnotic suggestion'. This may be interpreted in terms of redistribution of probability among the 'hypnosis' and 'mental effort' hypotheses: Increased probability of the latter enables rejection of the former. Lastly, it was found that the experience of an 'impossible phenomenon' does not increase the subjects' readiness to ascribe existence to other enigmatic phenomena: The mean subjective probability of these was about the same in the experimental and control conditions (36 per cent and 40 per cent respectively).

The data thus indicated that belief in physical object nonpermanence can be reactivated in educated adults. For that to be possible, however, certain conditions must be observed: first, the subjects have to observe the nonpermanence phenomenon that they cannot explain in the usual way; and, second, the actions and the instruction of the experimenter must make the acknowledgment of nonpermanence legitimate (for instance, through clothing it in the form of 'willpower' influence). The results, however, are restricted in many aspects, particularly with respect to the level of the subjects' education (university-educated or university students) and their cultural background. So far, there are no cross-cultural studies of object permanence in adults. However, as the belief in object permanence presupposes a belief in the existence of a magical causality (the possibility of influencing external physical events by sheer willpower or desire), there is some indirect evidence of a relationship between cultural background and the concept of object permanence in adults. Studies of 'magical thinking' have shown that one aspect of magical thinking was the subject's belief in the so-called 'paranormal phenomena', which included parapsychological abilities (the ability to transfer thoughts telepathically, to move material objects by 'willpower', ESP), unidentified flying objects, reincarnation of the soul, etc. (Zusne, 1985). Some of the studies revealed no differences in these beliefs between cultures (for example, in the United States and England), others obtained the opposite results, showing the relationship of certain beliefs (associated with magical childcare practices) to ethnic and socioeconomic factors (see Zusne and Jones, 1982).

Among the factors influencing paranormal beliefs (e.g. sex, age, urban or rural habitation, economic status, religion, etc.), *personality factors* are mentioned as well. While pointing out that the data should be treated with caution, Zusne and Jones (1982) nevertheless conclude that 'it would appear that variables related to feelings of uncertainty, the belief that one's fate is controlled externally, and social marginality may represent the composite dimension that often facilitates the development of paranormal beliefs' (1982, p. 190). According to Zusne and Jones, these feelings might be facilitated, among other factors, by authoritarianism, externalization, life change and/or emotional instability.

Taking this indirect evidence into consideration, one might hypothesize that such variables operate not only 'inside' a certain individual, but also on the interindividual and cultural levels as well. This means that in those societies that undergo a relatively stable and continuous development and that have uninterrupted democratic traditions allowing people to believe that they have control over their own lives, the above mentioned variables should have much less influence on an individual than in a society going through a period of social instability and uncertainty. If such variables of predictability and security somehow have an influence on the magical beliefs of adults, one could expect them to correspond to different object permanence beliefs. In order to test this hypothesis one needs to look for adequate societal contexts which serve as representatives of these two types of societies. We assumed that Germany and the Soviet Union might be chosen as such societal contexts.* There is no doubt that Soviet society is undergoing crucial and painful changes. The official ideology which has dominated the Soviet peoples' behaviour for over seventy years and has monopolized the search for truth has faltered,

---

* The experiment was conducted in 1988 before the collapse of the Soviet Union.

nationalists riots and separatist tendencies in Soviet republics are threatening the very existence of the Soviety empire and the economy is collapsing – all of which is more than enough to create uncertainty and instability. It should also be mentioned that, in general, Soviet society historically has been extremely authoritarian and totalitarian.

Modern German society* is a complete contrast to the Soviet picture described above. Although Germany has also passed through a period of totalitarianism, this period was not as long as that in the case of the Soviet society. For over forty years, German society has enjoyed consistent economic growth, democratic development and cultural consolidation. If the factors of crisis or stability in a society do influence the tendency to accept or reject paranormal and magical beliefs, these beliefs should be expected to occur to a lesser extent in modern German culture than in the modern Soviet culture.

However, there is one more fundamental difference between the German and the Soviet cultures that might influence the attribution of existence to some nonpermanent phenomena, namely, attitude towards the Christian religious tradition. It is common knowledge that the suppression of traditional religious beliefs by official ideology was a part of Soviet history; as a result, a materialistic and atheistic outlook on the world asserted itself in the consciousness of the Soviet individual at an early age. In contrast, in Germany, religious traditions (Protestant in the North, Catholic in the South), have been strong. Despite the fact that in Germany individualism has contributed to a secularization of religious beliefs and a steady rise of 'post-materialistic' values (Meulemann, 1985), a religious education is still an inseparable part of most Germans' socialization experience (in school and church).

Bearing this difference in mind, one might expect German and Soviet subjects to evaluate those nonpermanent phenomena which are rooted in the Christian religious tradition ('existence of a Supreme Being which created our universe and is responsible for its laws' and 'immortality of the human soul') differently from those which are independent of this tradition.

Indeed, the three hypotheses about the causes of the transformation of the postage stamp proposed by the experimenter ('willpower', 'hypnotic suggestion' and 'trick') and some of the mysterious nonpermanent

---

* The former West Germany is meant here.

phenomena ('UFO', 'parapsychological phenomena', 'Abominable snowman', 'Loch Ness monster') are not linked to Christian religious beliefs and can be easily understood in terms of scientific thinking or in terms of 'magical/supernatural beliefs' which contradicts the traditional Christian outlook.

The former group will be labelled 'religion-linked phenomena'; we assume that these phenomena will be attributed a higher degree of existence in German culture because of its uninterrupted religious tradition. The latter group of nonpermanent phenomena will be referred to as 'religion-independent'; it may be expected to have a higher probability of existence in the Soviet culture because of the influence of emotional instability and distress originating from the crisis situation in Soviet society.

With all this in mind, we repeated the experiment on object permanence and paranormal beliefs conducted with Soviet adults (described above) with a German group.* The aim of the study was to compare the explanatory behaviour of Soviet subjects with that of German subjects in the 'nonpermanence-provoking' experimental situations and to compare their beliefs in the existence of enigmatic 'paranormal' phenomena.

Sixty subjects participated in the experiment. Most of them were German students from Konstanz University, others former university graduates. Their ages ranged from 19 to 43 with a mean age 24.2.

The procedure of the German study followed strictly that of the study carried out in Moscow (see above).

The data revealed some similarities as well as some substantial differences between the Russian and the German groups with respect to the attribution of permanence. (Total scores across conditions are shown in Figure 2.3.)

Thus, the subjects of both samples state unanimously that the physical object in their perceptual field really exists, and they give the same reasons (clarity and distinctiveness of visual impression, past experience with the object); however, German subjects did not go beyond giving these reasons whereas some Russian subjects used the other person's experience (intersubjectivity) as well.

---

* The study was undertaken in Germany in co-operation with Gisela Trommsdorff (see Subbotsky and Trommsdorff, 1991).

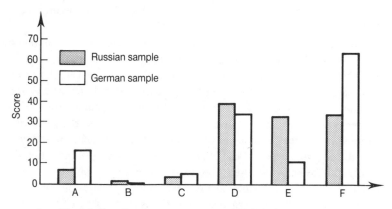

A subjects believe that the postage stamp, which is in the box, changed its appearance after the influence of willpower (MSP, %)
B perceptive identification (proportion of subjects).
C cognitive identification (proportion of subjects).
D subjects believe that the object was changed as a result of the experimenter's willpower (MSP, %)
E subjects believe that they were in a hypnotic state (MSP, %)
F subjects think that it was a trick (MSP, %)

Figure 2.3 Total scores of mastering the nonpermanence phenomena

Another important difference was the absence of the 'perceptive iden-tification' phenomenon in the German subjects, which took place in the Russian subjects under the 'reconstruction' condition. 'Cognitive identi-fication' took place to an equal extent in both samples, with the German subjects as well as the Russian subjects giving cognitive identification responses significantly more often under 'destruction' condition than under the 'transformation' condition – a fact that Subbotsky (1991) tried to explain through a 'law of entropy'.

The spontaneous explanations from both cultural groups were in general alike, though in a few cases Russian subjects suggested that the experimenter had manipulated their consciousness. The estimations of the three hypotheses given by the experimenter about the causes of the changes to the postage stamp revealed indirect differences between the German and Russian participants. For the German subjects, the 'trick' hypothesis was significantly more probable than the 'hypnosis' hypo-thesis, which got a very low MSP; for the Russian subjects, there was no such difference, all three hypotheses getting approximately equal MSPs.

The data do not show that the two cultural samples rely upon the 'nonpermanence rule' to different degrees in their assessment of the possibility of nonpermanence of a physical object. However, the results do reveal some differences on a dimension that can be designated as 'self- vs. other people-orientation': Russian subjects were more prone to use another person's experience and were less ready to trust their own per- ceptions than German subjects were. This tendency was represented in some Russian participants' use of another person's perception when dis- cussing the reasons for their conviction regarding a physical object's existence, and in the phenomenon of perceptive identification, and in the stronger feeling they experienced of their own suggestability (e.g. the spontaneous hypothesis that the experimenter had changed their percep- tion, high MSP of 'hypnosis' hypothesis). In contrast, German subjects were generally more suspicious in the experimental situation; they were less willing to admit that their consciousness had been manipulated and more inclined to trust their own perception. However, these observations rely upon indirect evidence only and must be treated with caution.

More clear-cut differences were revealed in the subjects' assessment of the existence of the nonpermanent mysterious phenomena (total scores across conditions are shown in Figure 2.4). As expected, the Russian subjects attributed a significantly higher MSP to the religion- independent phenomena's existence ('UFO', 'abominable snowman', 'Loch Ness monster') than did the German subjects; in contrast, the MSPs the German subjects gave to religion-linked phenomena ('Supreme Being' and 'Immortality of the human soul') significantly exceeded those given by the Russian subjects. The only exception was for the 'parapsychological phenomena', which got approximately equal MSPs in both cultural groups.

The different attitudes of Russian and German subjects to these two groups of enigmatic nonpermanent phenomena were also revealed in the results of the correlational analysis. In Russian subjects, the religion- linked phenomena composed an isolated cluster, which may be inter- preted as evidence of an attitude of alienation towards these phenomena, whereas in German subjects, religion-linked phenomena were integrated into the whole structure of 'paranormal beliefs'. At the same time, in both cultural groups, high 'trick' hypothesis estimations were indicators of a generally sceptical attitude on the part of the subject towards 'paranormal

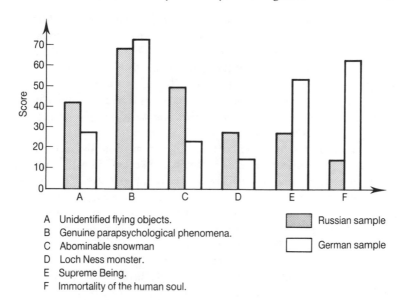

A Unidentified flying objects.
B Genuine parapsychological phenomena.
C Abominable snowman
D Loch Ness monster.
E Supreme Being.
F Immortality of the human soul.

Russian sample

German sample

Figure 2.4 Total mean subjective probability of unusual phenomena

phenomena' and high scores given to the 'willpower' hypothesis indicated the subject's belief in the existence of 'parapsychological phenomena' (see Subbotsky and Trommsdorf, 1991).

In sum, the study does not reveal significant differences in the estimation but rather in the explanation of nonpermanent phenomena (change of a physical object) observed by German and Russian participants. The hypothesis about the role of cultural factors in the attribution of existence of various paranormal phenomena has gained support. In a society undergoing a series of crucial and painful changes, a higher probability of existence is attributed to paranormal phenomena than in a society enjoying the conditions of economic and social stability. This, however, is relevant only to those nonpermanent phenomena that are not rooted in traditional religious beliefs; religion-linked phenomena are assessed as being more reliable in a culture with stabler religious traditions than in a more atheistically-oriented culture.

The studies described above aimed to distinguish the conditions under which preschool children and adults could believe in object nonpermanence; namely, to the *first problem* stated at the beginning of this section.

These studies showed that the single fact of the demonstration of object nonpermanence which a person could not explain was not enough in order to distort the person's belief in object permanence. This belief, however, could be weakened if the other person (in this case, the experimenter) expressed his belief in the possibility of nonpermanence.

The next study concerns the *second problem*. It aimed to examine *which psychological processes could be interrupted by the observation of physical object nonpermanence*.

In particular, one hypothetical possibility stems from the fact that an instance of object discontinuity is not an isolated event. As with any other event, an instance of object nonpermanence occupies a certain position in a continuous temporal chain of events, as well as occupying a definite position in space (i.e. it happens 'somewhere', in a certain place surrounded by other objects). In so far as an event of object nonpermanence is theoretically impossible within the physical universe and, nevertheless, *is observed*, the sudden disappearance of an object creates a dangerous rupture in the spatiotemporal continuum which threatens its very continuity. However, the nonpermanence event can easily be reinterpreted and presented as a normal physical event if the discontinuity it creates is shifted from the real physical world into the subjective world of an individual. For example, if the nonpermanence event is preceded by a short distraction of the subject's attention, the subject could reinterpret the event of object nonpermanence as an ordinary trick accomplished by the experimenter at the moment when subject's attention was diverted. Similarly, if the object disappears in a certain place, the subject can save his or her belief in object permanence by assuming that the object has been secretly concealed in this place so that it cannot be perceived. Thus, discontinuity of a material object is replaced by discontinuity or limitedness of the subject's attention.

However, subjects may be confronted with a more complex situation when their attention is distracted *not before, but after* the event of object nonpermanence. In this case the shift of discontinuity from the physical world to the subjective world is still possible, but now it requires a change in the temporal order of physical events; namely, subjects must allow that they had been distracted before the nonpermanent event. By the same token, if the objects that disappeared in a certain place *cannot be found in this place despite all the subjects' efforts to find it*, the subjects must allow that the object is somewhere else, thus violating the spatial order of the physical world (the fundamental assumption that the object that was hidden in a certain place and was not subsequently displaced must be in this place and cannot be in some other place).

Of course, these disturbances in the subjects' memory and reasoning about temporal and spatial order of the events might not be perceived by the subjects as violations. The change in temporal order may happen without the subjects' awareness of it, and the change in the object's spatial location may be rationalized by the subjects as a result of a simple displacement. However, it was assumed here that these disturbances in memory and reasoning would not happen if the subjects were not confronted with the unexplainable event.

The present experiment dealt with just these problems. It aimed to determine to what extent the real temporal and spatial order of the events which constitute a background for the nonpermanence phenomena could be violated in the memory and reasoning of adults in order to preserve their strong belief in permanence of physical objects (Subbotsky, 1992).

As in our previous work, in this study (in Experiment 1) subjects observed the unexplainable phenomena (instances of material objects' discontinuity). However, in so far as this time we were interested not in the conditions which might provoke subjects to believe in object nonpermanence, but in the hypotheses and explanations that the subjects might produce in order to conserve their beliefs in object permanence, the pattern of the experiment was changed.

First of all we excluded the 'willpower' manipulations which could provoke subjects to believe in 'parapsychological' influence; in this experiment subjects simply observed the nonpermanence phenomena. The major aim was to determine how the subjects would recollect the temporal and spatial succession of the events which led up to the nonpermanence phenomena.

First, it might be expected that the event which had happened in reality *before* the unexplainable phenomenon would be remembered and recalled by the subjects as one that happened *after* the unexplainable event, if this change in the temporal succession of the events could help the subjects to maintain their belief in object permanence (hypothesis 1 – *the reversal of the temporal order of the event*); in order to prove that the change in the temporal order of the events is caused by the observation of an unexplainable event, the subjects' recollections of the events which preceded and followed the unexplainable event should be compared with the recollections of the same events by the subjects who did not observe any unusual events.

Second, the site in which the unexplainable event had happened (a privileged place) might lose its privileged meaning if it could help the subjects to conserve their beliefs in object permanence. Contrary to ordinary logic the subjects would believe that the object that disappeared (appeared) in the box and was not subsequently (previously) displaced (placed in) is (or had been) located outside the box (hypothesis 2 – *the distortion of the spatial order of the events*).

Third, it might be assumed that distortions of both types will depend upon the 'salience' of the unusual event. They will happen more often if the unusual event that the subject observed is more salient (i.e. has no alternative plausible explanation) and less often if the unusual event is less salient (hypothesis 3 – *a positive relation between the frequency of distortions in subjects' memory and the 'salience' of the unexplainable event*). In order to check this assumption the subjects' accounts about the unusual events of various salience should be compared.

Two extreme cases of nonpermanence were taken as unexplainable events in this experiment. The complete disappearance of a physical object (a piece of paper) and the creation of a physical object (either a piece of paper or a postage stamp) 'from nothing'.

The subjects were sixty students from Lancaster University (England) (age range 18–40 years), most of them were native English speakers. Ten men and ten women participated in each of the three conditions. The general scheme of the experiment was basically the same as in the previous experiments with adult subjects; however, after the subject answered the first set of core questions the experimenter did not attempt to influence the box with his 'willpower', instead the subject was asked to fetch a toy truck, which had been placed in the far corner of the room behind the subject at a distance approximately 3–4 m away. The aim of this request was to discover whether the subject would try to use this rupture in his or her stream of consciousness in order to explain the unexpected disappearance (appearance) of a material object (e.g. by saying that the experimenter took the object out of (put it into) the box when the subject went to get the truck and was not watching the table).

The subject was then asked to put everything that he or she could see on the table in the empty box and close the lid. There were two experimental conditions and one control condition. In the 'appearance' and in the control condition, except for the box, there was only a postage stamp on the table; in the 'disappearance' condition there was also a scrap of paper. After the subject answered the second set of core questions and made necessary probability estimates, he or she was instructed to remove everything from the box and to put it on the table. On opening the box in the 'control' and 'disappearance' conditions the subject would find 'the same' postage stamp (in reality the other one that had been hidden between the metal plate and the wall of the box) but no other objects. In the 'appearance' condition the subject would find the postage stamp and either a piece of paper or (for a half of the subjects) another (bigger) postage stamp.

In the course of the ensuing conversation the experimenter put a further set of core questions, and among them the following ones: Have you been attentive through all the experiment or was there a moment when your attention was diverted? How do you think this scrap of paper could disappear (appear)? Now try to remember, what was the order?: Did you first bring me the toy truck and then put the object(s) into the box, or did you put the object(s) into the box and then fetch me the toy truck? The subjects were then asked to give probability estimates for the first (right) and for the second (wrong) hypothesis.

As expected, none of the subjects ignored the permanence rule in their spontaneous explanations of the unusual phenomena. On the contrary, trying to save their beliefs in object permanence by all means the subjects put under question that all of the three necessary conditions of object permanence had been met. Either the object was thought to lack stability and solidity (some of the subjects assumed that it was made of special material that dissolves in darkness) or the manner in which it went out of the perceptual field was supposed to be destructive (a chemical in the box dissolves the paper). Finally, the subjects assumed that their attention had been diverted and the object was removed from (put in) the box at that moment.

The last explanation was the most interesting one. It goes without saying that the rupture in the subjects' attention could have been either a result of a certain abnormal cause (hypnosis, illusion) or it was an ordinary distraction. Since the subjects gave very low MSPs for these abnormal causes they could not rely upon them in their explanations of what had happened with the object. In contrast, the hypothesis that the object had been extracted (put in) at the moment of a natural break in the subjects' attention (when they went to fetch the toy at the experimenter's request) was accepted by many subjects willingly. About half the subjects invented this hypothesis independently or in the course of the conversation with the experimenter. But this hypothesis implicitly included the

Foundations of the mind

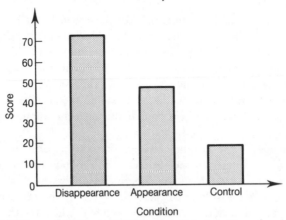

Figure 2.5 Mean subjective probabilities by subjects in Experiment 1 for the wrong temporal succession of the events (first the subjects put the object(s) in the box and then they went to pick up the toy)

change of the temporal succession of the events: The real order must have been substituted by the one that made it possible for the experimenter imperceptibly to manipulate the box (the subjects put the objects into the box and *after that* they went to pick up the truck). It was exactly what happened: a number of subjects (25 total) ascribed more than 50 per cent probability to the wrong temporal succession (see Figure 2.5). Only 11 subjects (7 of them in the control condition) totally rejected the possibility for the wrong succession to happen.

Since the MSPs given for the wrong succession of the events in both experimental conditions signficantly exceeded the MSP given for the wrong succession in the control condition, this typical mistake could not have been caused solely by the insufficiency of subjects' memory: in all the conditions approximately the same time passed between the moment of closing the box with a set of objects and the end of the question about the succession of the events (4.55 min. in the 'disappearance' condition, 4.40 min. in the 'appearance' condition and 4.54 min. in the control condition). This fact confirms hypothesis 1, according to which the unexplainable phenomenon (violation of object permanence) creates disturbances in subjects' memory through changing the temporal succession of the events.

The results also confirmed hypothesis 3 – the assumption that the distortion of temporal order depends on the salience of an unusual phenomenon. As expected, the MSP given for the wrong succession was smallest in the control condition, it was significantly larger in the 'appearance' condition, and it was the largest in the 'disappearance' condition. However, the role of the type of object that appeared (a postage stamp v. a scrap of paper) proved to be insignificant.

Hypothesis 2 (predicting a change in the subordination of various parts of space) also gained support in the experiment. Having found no piece of paper in the box in the 'disappearance condition', the subjects tended to look for it under the box, then under the table and within the experimenter's reach. Later, many of the subjects acknowledged that the object could be anywhere outside the box, thus violating the fundamental assumption that underlies the organization of physical space (if the object was put in a certain place and was not subsequently displaced it (or its remnants) must be in this place and not elsewhere). As one subject put it, '. . . since the object is not in the box, it can be anywhere – in this truck, on your person or on the chair under you . . . I can assume that with equal probabilities'. The strong correlation between the subjects who recollected the wrong temporal succession and those who produced the 'object being outside the box' hypothesis makes it very probable that both phenomena are consequences of the same cause – the person's desire to explain the material object disappearance in a natural way.

The results of Experiment 1, however, do not answer several questions which might be important for understanding the mechanisms that help subjects to conserve their belief in object permanence. First of all, the question is left open whether a real rupture in the subjects' consciousness is a necessary condition in order for the distortions described to occur?

Indeed, it might be assumed that since in the two experimental conditions there was a real rupture in the subjects' consciousness (the moment when the subjects went to pick up the toy truck) when the experimenter could manipulate the box and the objects without being observed by the subjects, the subjects used this fact (consciously or unconsciously) as a plausible explanation for the nonpermanence phenomena. Once this explanation was accepted, the distortions in the temporal succession and spatial hierarchy of events appeared in the subjects' memory. However, these distortions might not have happened if the rupture did not occur, e.g. if the subjects did not go to pick up the toy but just observed this action being done by somebody else. The position of *an observer* would differ from the position of *an active subject* in that the former would keep both the subject and the experimenter permanently in his or her visual field and, therefore, would have no obvious reasons to change the temporal succession of the events as it would the active subject. In other words, the question is *whether the nonpermanence phenomenon is strong enough to cause distortions not only in active subjects' consciousness, but in the consciousness of observers as well.*

The second question concerns the stability of the distortions described, namely, are the changes in temporal succession and in the spatial hierarchy of the events relatively stable in time or do they only happen under the influence of an immediate situation? If the second were true, then a few days after the experiment the spontaneous work of the subjects' consciousness would restore the real temporal succession of the events in the subjects' memory or somehow change the original subjects' judgements produced during the experiment.

The third problem was to see whether the deformation of the real temporal and spatial relationships between the events under the influence of object nonpermanence is a culturally invariant phenomenon, provided that the experiment is conducted in a different European culture.

To address these questions Experiment 2 was conducted.* Forty subjects took part in the experiment, all of them were native German speakers. Most of the subjects were students of German universities, the rest were educated to university degree level. Subjects' ages ranged from 21 to 63.

The procedure of the experiment was the same as in Experiment 1 in the 'disappearance' condition, with two differences. First, in this experiment two persons were tested together: one of them was asked to be 'a subject', and the other to be 'an observer'. The latter was asked to watch everything carefully and to answer the experimenter's questions. The subject sat at a table facing the experimenter (as in Experiment 1), the observer sat to one side. All the core questions that were put to the subject were next put to the observer as well, with the aim of determining whether the absence of a rupture in visual control over the situation would reduce the distortions in the temporal and spatial relationships of the events in the observer's consciousness in comparison with the distortions in the subject's consciousness.

* This experiment was conducted at the Department of Social Sciences of Konstanz University (Germany) during the author's fellowship granted by Alexander von Humboldt Foundation (Germany).

Second, two or three days after the experiment the subject and the observer were asked to retell everything they could remember of the experiment. They were again asked to make probability estimates for the succession of the events in time and for the three hypotheses provided by the experimenter. The objective of this session was to learn whether certain spontaneous work of the participants' consciousness would restore or transform the real temporal succession of the events in the participants' memory and whether it would somehow influence the subjects' and observers' assessments.

The results of this experiment were very much like those obtained in Experiment 1 in the 'disappearance' condition. There were no differences either in the spontaneous hypotheses or in reasons given by the German subjects and observers to justify their judgements about the existence of material objects.

The results showed that the phenomenon of changing the temporal succession and the spatial hierarchy of the events under the influence of object nonpermanence occurred in subjects' and in observers' consciousness to an equal extent.

One might assume this to be the result of conformity. Indeed, in so far as the observers were asked the same questions as were the subjects, they might merely have reproduced the subjects' estimates. However, in this case a strong correlation must be expected between MSPs given by the subjects and those given by the observers. The nonsignificant correlation between MSPs given for the wrong succession by the subjects and by the observers who participated in the same experimental session ($r = 0.363$, $f > 0.05$) does not allow us to account for the high scores by observers to be simply a result of the reproduction of the subjects' estimates; rather, it shows that observers' assessments were given independently of those of the subjects'. The results testify, therefore, in favour of the assumption that *disruptions in the subjects' visual control over the situation were not a necessary condition for the distortions in their consciousness to occur. The observation of the object nonpermanence alone can create distortions in observers' consciousness.*

The fact that the subjects' assessment did not change in the delayed reproduction proves *the relative stability of the assessments.*

The absence of any significant cultural and gender differences shows *the invariance of the distortions that occur in the subjects' consciousness under the influence of an observation of a physical object nonpermanence.* The cultural differences between the MSPs of the hypothesis that the postage stamp that had been closed in the box disappeared from the world does not directly concern the phenomenon of object nonpermanence; rather, it shows that male German subjects were basically more suspicious that some destructive processes may have occurred in the box.

Concluding remarks

It seems quite possible that belief in the discontinuity of a material object and belief in the existence of enigmatic phenomena psychologically are two sides of the same coin. They might represent a specific desire of contemporary Europeans for unusual experiences that transcend the boundaries of everyday reality.* This notion finds some support in the fact that the subjects in one of the present studies (Russian sample) regularly expressed their desire to encounter mysterious or supernatural phenomena ('I would like this [transformation of the postage stamp] to be possible', 'I want to believe that these "unidentified flying objects" are from extraterrestrial civilizations', 'I want this phenomenon to exist because it broadens the limits of reality').

As opposed to the well-known 'need for new experiences' this 'need for the unusual' cannot be satisfied by accessing new information, but only by very unusual phenomena that transcend the boundaries of the natural.

It may be speculated that this 'need for the unusual' or 'transcendental need', in common with some other fundamental needs (such as the sexual drive, for example), is partially suppressed in modern rationalistic cultures. This unfulfilled need gives rise to the intensive interest many people in the industrialized world show in folk tales, myths, fantastic stories and mysterious phenomena, including extraterrestrial beings, extrasensory perception and many more.

Coming back to the problem of existence, one might recall René Descartes who was the first to propose methods of dealing with the reality of existence (Descartes, 1960). According to Descartes existence can only be ascertained with clear, distinct and unequivocal knowledge. From a

---

* Some hypothetical determinants of this desire have been analysed by Zusne (1985).

psychological point of view the Cartesian school of thought reflects the fundamental need for an individualistic mind to create its own representation of the universe in the individual's consciousness, freeing the world of dogmas and fantastic beliefs. But this is only one side of the ambivalent European personality. The other side is the desire to attribute existence to knowledge which is highly indeterminate and improbable, and by its very improbability pushes back the boundaries of the universe. This is what may be called the transcendental need. Closer investigation of this hypothetical need warrants further research.

Nevertheless, the results of this study clearly indicated that belief in the possibility of nonpermanence of physical objects is not unique to the minds of young infants but can also be found in preschool childen and adults. These beliefs were revealed in such experimental conditions that they could not be accounted for merely by the subjects' unwillingness to contradict the expressed views of the experimenter: the children were left to act alone in the absence of the experimenter and, in the case of adults, the hypothesis of 'willpower' influence was only one of three possible interpretations.

However, it should be stressed again that belief in object nonpermanence can be released in adults only under the combined influence of a nonpermanence phenomenon and specific actions of the experimenter who (at least indirectly) admits the possibility of nonpermanence. Without such combination adults' belief in object permanence cannot be undermined. As the last two experiments showed, adult subjects actively refuse to acknowledge the reality of nonpermanence even if they observe them. A particular form of this refusal is a transformation of temporal and spatial order of the events that surround the nonpermanence phenomenon in such a way that enables the subjects to shift a phenomenon of object discontinuity from the physical world into the subjective world of the individual. Subjects are prone to make this transformation even if they have no obvious pretext for it (as was the case with observers in the last experiment). These transformations are relatively stable and invariant with respect to gender or nationality (German or English subjects).

One speculative implication of this result concerns a possibility that in the foreseeable future scientists can meet some phenomena incompatible even with the most fundamental physical laws. Although this possibility is extremely small, it cannot be excluded in principle. In fact, the 'behaviour' of certain entities on the subnuclear layer is reminiscent of the behaviour of a nonpermanent physical object. The results of such a meeting may be two-fold. On the one hand, this might result in some modifications in the description of physical objects, on the other hand, it may create a need to look more closely at our psychological habits and stereotypes in dealing with material objects. Our belief in the permanence of physical objects is one of these stereotypes; the other is a contemporary educated person's strong belief in physical causality.

Chapter 3

The ontogenesis of the causality notion

Emil Durkheim, Edward Taylor, James Frazer and Lucien Lévy-Brühl demonstrated long ago the crucial role of culture in the development of fundamental concepts such as the representation of causality, which appear to be astonishingly different in the so called 'primitive cultures' than the European. However, it remained unclear, (1) whether primitive people's belief in magical causality and nonpermanent objects was a natural result of their 'collective mind's' primitivity, or (2) it was constantly produced and conserved by the cultures because it had constructive and creative roles in these cultures.

At present, with the elaboration of the theory of accidental processes, and the new discoveries in the natural sciences (in particular, of the uncertainty principle or the dissipative structures: see Prigogine and Stengers, 1986), this question gains in importance. And another old problem is facing us again: What in the concept of the causal ties comes from the 'external world' and culture, and what proceeds from the active subject who is transforming the world?

It is my belief that any serious attempt to answer the questions inevitably faces problems of development. But before discussing this it might be helpful briefly to remind the reader of the notion of causality and the characteristics that distinguish it from a correlation or an accidental coincidence.

It is generally assumed that causal ties are the kind of ties between discreet events (phenomena, states) A and B, where event A is a necessary and sufficient condition of the emergence of event B and precedes the former in time (see Chapter 1). We shall also distinguish between psychological and natural causality. *Psychological causality* signifies that cause A for event B is the subject him/herself. This can be subdivided into (1) psychophysical causality (A – the thought and the experience of the subject; B – the movements of his/her body); (2) magical causality (A – the thought of the subject; B – an event in the outer world); (3) artificialistic causality (A – the corporeal action of the subject, directed at the external object; B – the transformation of the object). *Natural causality* refers to the causal ties between the two events which are external to the subject; within this type of causal connections event A is either a phenomenal cause (it produces B without the subject supplying any rational construction to understand the connection), or a physical cause (the subject has the rational construction available to trace the causal connection).

It is not my intention to discuss here causality problems in a cross-cultural perspective, however interesting that may be. What is important at this point is that the first of the two above-mentioned views has been accepted in developmental psychology.

Thus, Piaget in one of his most brilliant studies (Piaget, 1937a) argues that the development of causality and object permanence in a child goes through a series of stages. In stages 1 and 2 (0–3 months) the child's universe is not perceived as something separate. At these stages there are no stable discrete objects, outer space or objective time; any physical or psychological causality is absent. There is a simple feeling or sensation by the infant of its subjectivity (effort, action, demand) and its result (e.g. a thumb in the mouth) in an integral whole, or, as Piaget put it, a sensation of '*efficacité*' of action.

At the third stage (3–7 months) the difference between Ego and Non-Ego is still absent, but infants develop a primary idea of the link between intention and the effect. Nevertheless, the child does not yet distinguish its hand from the object it touches, and perceives the external effect as a direct consequence of the intention (the magical causality).

The fourth stage about 8–12 months) is characterized by a partial objectivization of the causality, which is manifested, for instance, in urging the adult to act by means of manipulation with the adult's hand. Thus, children no longer regard their actions as the only source of activity, but ascribe the ability of action to the body of another person or a thing. So Jacqueline (Piaget's daughter), at the age of nine months, no longer grasped and shook the watch on the chain upon seeing it but delicately touched it with her finger, trying to encourage its 'independent' movement. However, this kind of objectivization is limited: children fail to distinguish outward objects from their own activity and suppose that their spontaneous action occurs due only to their initiative.

At the fifth stage (12–17 months) children demonstrate in their actions the understanding of physical causality for the first time. Thus they manipulate objects relying on their own 'logic', but not on the logic of its body, e.g. they put objects on the inclined plane and observe them rolling down.

At this stage the 'Ego' and the world, psychological and physical causality become separated. But for all that, children are still unable to imagine the causal connection between the events in the mental plane, but only realize it in concretely perceived things.

Only at the sixth stage (from 18 months) does the ability to represent causality appear. It manifests itself as: (1) the ability to reconstruct the cause proceeding from the consequence only; (2) the ability to foresee the consequence proceeding from the visible cause in the case when children have not come across this consequence in their previous experience. Now the universe is no longer perceived by children as 'a series of births and deaths', but as a continuing process, a stream of causes and consequences, the beginnings and the ends of which are going into the future and the past.

However, in their verbal judgement, children of 4–5 years suffer a regression towards the level of the magic and phenomenalistic causality (Piaget, 1927). In his studies of children's judgements on the causes of natural phenomena (wind, the movement of the celestial bodies, the waves on the surface of a lake, etc.), on the functioning of engines (bicycle, motorcycle engine), Piaget distinguished a number of typical 'precausal' responses: magical, finalistic, artificialistic, pseudo-scientific. Not until they reach adolescence are children able to give purely physical explanations.

A specific aspect of children's reasoning on the causes of the physical phenomena is animism (Piaget, 1927). Initially, children ascribe life and conscience (the ability to feel, understand . . .) to all objects, next to moving objects, and then to the object endowed with the spontaneous movement (wind, river); in the last stages life is associated only with animals and people. Characteristically, with respect to artificial objects, animism is manifested more weakly than towards natural phenomena.

In this fascinating picture there is one characteristic feature: according to Piaget, at the beginning of development, children's minds lack physical causality and are entirely ruled by magic and nonpermanence, not because of some 'cultural influences' (which are minimal at this age) but simply because of their primitive, assimilative *nature*. This 'primitive mind', however, comes under the steady influence of culture, and children, through their numerous activities and communications with objects and people, eventually acquire the concepts of physical causality and permanence of objects (at first, on the level of sensorimotor actions, later, on the level of verbal judgements).

This position is far from being isolated. For instance, Vygotsky's view on the development of spontaneous and scientific concepts differs from Piaget's with respect to the sources of the spontaneous concepts, which are more 'social' and 'cultural' in their origins (Vygotsky, 1982). However, in his view, as in Piaget's, spontaneous concepts still reign in children's minds at the start of mental development; although they never disappear, they are progressively 'forced out' of the mind under the influence of education.

Common to these most influential psychological perspectives of the twentieth century is this idea of a steady progress in the mental development of children, the logic of 'cultural optimism', which could be traced to the great rationalistic theories in the eighteenth and nineteenth centuries. According to this logic, psychological relics, such as belief in magical causality and in nonpermanence of a physical object, however strong at the start of mental development, are inevitably doomed to extinction or, at least, to exercising a submissive and unimportant role in the human mind. Nevertheless, in recent decades this optimistic 'replacement model' has been increasingly questioned. This challenge has taken the form of numerous demonstrations of the outstanding abilities of young children to understand physical causality.

Thus, Raspe (1924) asked childen aged 7–11 to explain the phenomenon of successive light contrast. Although the children could not give correct explanations, they did not reveal any obvious animistic tendencies. Similar data were reported by Huang (1930), who studied explanations of certain mysterious phenomena (mostly tricks) by children aged 4–11. In these and subsequent studies (Zaporozhets and Lukov, 1941; Venger, 1958) preschool children's causal judgements were found to be of a global or phenomenalistic character; but they explained unknown events in a 'naturalistic' manner rather than in a 'magical' or 'artificialistic' way. Kun (1978) showed that even three-year-old children in most cases would understand the unidirectional character of causal connections. Bullock and Gelman (1979) reported data showing that three-year-olds could understand simple mechanical causality, although the children could not give satisfactory verbal explanations. Three-year-old children's competence in understanding mechanical causal ties was confirmed in other studies (Schultz *et al.*, 1986), although limitations of this understanding were revealed as well (Keil, 1979; Bullock, 1985).

It was also found that this early competence was basically nonverbal: replications of Piaget's verbal 'clinical' tests produced concordant results (Laurendeau and Pinard, 1962; Schwartz, 1980; Carey, 1985). It was in children's explanations and not in their actions that animism flourished (Williamson *et al.*, 1982; Hagleitner, 1983; Beveridge and Davies, 1983), and even in explanations it faded away if children were tested with refined methodology (Bullock, 1984, 1985). As for nonverbal tests, children as young as two showed an ability to distinguish between animate and inanimate objects (Golinkoff *et al.*, 1984); but the data that were, perhaps, most challenging for 'linear perspective' came from recent developments in studies of infancy. Using the habituation–dishabituation paradigm, Ball showed that nine-month-old infants could differentiate the so-called 'direct launching' from 'launching without collision' (see Leslie, 1982) – the phenomenon described earlier by Michotte (1962) in his studies with adult subjects. Persisting in this line of investigation, Leslie showed the ability of even younger infants (5 months) to detect 'direct launching' and its specific quality – a spatiotemporal continuity between causes and consequences (Leslie, 1982, 1984a, b).

Leslie proposed the idea that human perception has a specific 'modular' character (Leslie, 1986). A 'module' is a specific, formal structure immanently inserted into consciousness, which is automatically applied to the coming sensory information. It seems quite reasonable that such modules should reveal themselves very early in ontogenesis, which the author's experiments persuasively demonstrate with respect to the 'causality module'. The function of the module is to 'get development off the ground', to set the process of understanding physical causality into motion.

The data introduce certain essential corrections into the picture of the development in children of notions of causality as they were put forward by Piaget. The new methods of investigation provide the grounds for believing that even very young infants are capable of perceiving certain connections between moving objects as a causal tie and distinguishing the latter as a specific quality. Basically, the data are consistent with the view of the development of fundamental structures of the mind as a gradual distinction between categorical oppositions. However, the data challenged the 'replacement model' in one single direction, showing that the idea of physical causality is not alien to very young children and even to 5-month-old infants. Nevertheless, the 'coexistence model' assumes that the contrary must be true as well; animistic and magical causality must exercise its influence upon the behaviour of preschool and school-aged children, and even adults. This assumption may encourage the search for the conditions under which magic can still be a reality for older children and which can determine their verbal and practical behaviour in various domains of consciousness.

The 'natural' and 'animistic' modes of assimilation of reality in children

Contrary to investigators who think that the 'animistic' and 'natural causality' approaches to the explication of physical phenomena are two *successive phases* in the development of a child's thought (Raspe, 1924; Piaget, 1927, 1937a; Tul'viste, 1981) – i.e. that the second occurs *after* the first, coexists with it for some time and then begins to predominate – we suggest that the animistic and the natural science modes are in categorical opposition to one another and that the child's conception of them emerges in his or her consciousness *at the same time*. Viewing the problem in this way eliminates the difficulty of explaining the transition from animistic thinking (which a priori cannot be broken down by experience because 'experience' itself already is based on a notion of scientific causality) to natural causality.

These ways of assimilating the world, learned as oppositions, coexist in different domains of a child's everyday experience (play, dreams, imagination, stories, daily reality) as well as *within single domains*. However, the 'psychological status' of these modes of thought is different.

Thus, in the domain of everyday reality, a child who has assimilated the above categorical opposition has legitimately mastered the natural scientific mode of explaining events. This mode entails two basic postulates: (1) *a nonliving object is incapable of spontaneous self-display* (for example, a toy rabbit cannot be transformed into a live rabbit; one object cannot be arbitrarily transformed into another; an immobile object cannot start to move by itself without a 'push'); (2) *it is impossible to exert a* *force upon an object directly through thought* (by 'magical words', incantation, orders, etc.). According to our hypothesis, at the legitimate level of assimilating phenomena (for example, in the course of conversations with an adult), a child will implicitly or explicitly adhere to these postulates in everyday reality. But, in this *same domain of living practice*, the opposite mode of assimilating the world, which requires these postulates to be violated (belief in the possibility of spontaneous transformations and magical forces) must exist in the child in a subordinate and latent form.*

To prove this hypothesis, a procedure must be developed in which the same phenomenon in everyday reality will be assimilated by the child in different ways: in one case, on the basis of natural explanations, and in the other, on the basis of 'animistic' explanations. The first case is more probable in a situation of *verbal behaviour*, i.e. when children will explain to the experimenter the causes of a physical phenomenon presented to them in the form of a story or a fairy tale. It may be assumed that in this situation children who have assimilated the opposition 'natural v. magical' will adhere to 'natural' causes (though they may be incorrect from an adult's point of view) even in explaining unintelligible phenomena: in such a situation they will be under the supervision of the adult and be required to use legitimate (i.e. scientific) norms of reasoning, and will have no interest in using the contrasting animistic method of explanation.

---

* In particular, this belief shows up in certain aspects of a child's fear. Thus, one four-year-old child we observed developed a fear of a 'bamzeli', a magical monster who came to his bed when the child was ready to go to sleep and was left alone in a dark room. The boy himself found a way to 'neutralize' the monster: he would roll up the edge of his blanket and hold the tube he had formed in his hand: he believed that so long as he held this tube, the monster would not appear. Later, the child would take other, similar objects in his hand in place of the tube, and would peacefully fall asleep with them. It is also not superfluous to point out that such magical forms of accommodating to reality exist in acute situations in adults as well, indeed, even in highly educated people. Recourse to magical acts (knock on wood, spitting over one's shoulder) may take place in both explicit and implicit reduced form, with elements of irony with regard to these acts, which nevertheless are very persistent and easily coexist alongside the natural scientific mode of explaining the world in the sphere of everyday life. Furthermore, it may be assumed that forms of magic fulfil a useful function in the mental life of mankind, that of *mediating and dominating* the area of mental reality that is beyond the control of rational scientific methods (fear of death, misfortune, suppressed desires, etc.).

For children to use the animistic method not only in the sphere of life practice in which they imagine them to be the legitimate norm (story, game) but also in that of everyday reality, two conditions must be met: (1) the children's behaviour must be free of external monitoring (i.e. children should be 'alone' with the phenomenon), and (2) the 'animistic' assimilation of the phenomenon must be significantly motivated. This experimental situation is also critical for our hypothesis: if the child really does have an animistic explanation of phenomena in latent form, in this situation it should show up in explicit form by altering the child's real behaviour, i.e. his or her practical assimilation of the real physical phenomenon previously presented in the form of a story, in a characteristic way. If, on the other hand, the child does not have the animistic way of explaining things in the sphere of everyday reality, in this situation, as in the sphere of verbal behaviour, he or she will assimilate the phenomenon in a rational manner based on the presumptions of natural science.

In one of these experiments (Subbotsky, 1985) we tried to determine conditions under which preschool children could believe that it was possible to exert force upon an object directly by means of thought. In the first condition of the experiment (verbal behaviour) 4- to 6-year-old children were first asked two questions to determine whether they admitted the possibility of the direct action of thought on an object in the sphere of everyday reality: (1) Can drawings be changed into what they depict? (2) Can a drawing of an elephant be changed into a real elephant if you say a magic word?

The children were then told the story of 'The magic box'. The hero of the story, the little girl Masha, receives a box for a present; the box has the magical capacity to transform drawings of objects into the objects themselves. To do this it is necessary to put a drawing in the box and say the magic words 'Alpha beta gamma' aloud. At first Masha did not believe this, but when she tested the box, she became convinced of its magical properties.

Each subject of our experiment was asked to retell the story and then was asked: 'Why does the box transform the pictures into objects?' The purpose of this question was to determine whether the child admitted the possibility of the direct action of thought on an object within the structure of a story.

In the *second condition*, we studied the child's real behaviour without any external monitoring. A few days after the first series, the child was invited into the experimental room and asked: 'Do you want me to show you the same magic box that was given to Masha?' The experimenter would give the child a pretty box and drawings depicting a ring, a brooch, a cigarette lighter, a fountain pen, a spider and a wasp. He would then show the child some of these objects, which were supposed to have been obtained from the box, and say: 'I'm going out to do some things, and meanwhile you can play. If you want you can use the box – only don't forget that you have to say the magic words aloud; otherwise, the box can't hear them.' The experimenter told the child the magic words again and went out to observe the child's behaviour through an opening in a screen.

It was assumed that in this situation the child's behaviour would tell us enough to say whether or not there was an animistic presumption in the way he or she assimilated phenomena: (1) if at the 'background' level, i.e., at the level of latent 'subordinated' norms, the child admitted the possibility of direct action of thought on an object, in this particular situation he or she would try it out; (2) but if he or she did not admit this possibility, the child would assimilate the objects obtained by rational means: he or she would handle the box, the pictures, etc., since from the standpoint of natural causality attempts to transform a picture into an object would be meaningless.

Furthermore, if variant (1) was undertaken, two interpretations were possible: first, it could be assumed that the child's assimilation of the object spontaneously shifted into another sphere of living practice and that the child simply *pretended* that the box was a magic box; second, it might be assumed that this shift did not take place and that the child really did hope that the object would be transformed.

The differentiation of these hypotheses took place in a *post-experimental interview*. During this interview the experimenter, who by then had returned, would ask the child: 'Well, did you try to transform the pictures? Did you succeed?' 'Did you say the magic words aloud?' If the child had performed magical acts at a pretending level, and if he or she understood the conditions of the situation, he or she would not count on the transformation and hence would not be disappointed in the box. But if the child really did count on the effect, his or her statements about the box would contain elements of disappointment, and he or she would regard the lack of success of his or her actions as *failure*.

After the interview, the experimenter would sit for five minutes in the room and write without giving the child anything specific to do; this was designed to see whether the child would again attempt to transform the pictures in the presence of an adult or whether the external control would be conducive to cessation of the magical practice. This situation made up the third and last condition of the experiment (real behaviour under conditions of external control from an adult).

Results showed that all 5- and 6-year-olds and 75 per cent of 4-year-olds verbally denied the possibility of the direct action of thought on an object in the sphere of everyday reality in the initial part of the interview. When asked why, some either refused to give any arguments at all or 'argued' their negative answer simply by stating it ('It isn't transformed because it isn't transformed'); others pointed out the material of which the object was made ('A bottle can't be changed into a rabbit since it's made of glass; a drawing of an elephant can't be transformed into a living elephant because it's paper and it's drawn'). The most typical answer of the older children was to say that magic was impossible in real, everyday life ('Objects in a picture cannot be transformed since they are not magical; there's no magic in real life'). When then asked where magic could be found, they unanimously answered 'in stories'; some added 'in church', 'in cartoon films', 'at the cinema' etc.

In the situation of real behaviour with the absence of external control (second condition), about 90 per cent of the children in each age category

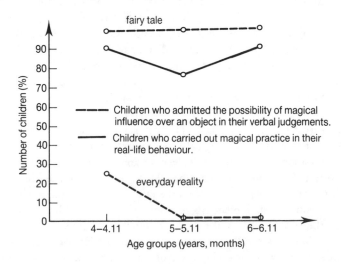

Figure 3.1 Children's behaviour in the 'Magic box' situation

tried to transform the pictures into the object (see Figure 3.1). Usually, when left alone in the room a child would put the drawings of the wasp and spider aside ('I don't want a spider and a wasp; they're terrible'), would place a drawing they liked in the box (the girls, the ring or the brooch; the boys, the cigarette lighter or the fountain pen), close it, and pronounce the 'magic words'; many of them would make a gesture over the box or make circular movements as they pronounced the words. They would then open the box, and look with bewilderment at the drawing, shrug their shoulders, or exclaim with surprise: 'It didn't happen! The drawing's still there!' Having looked for the object in the box, the child would usually place the picture in again and repeat his or her attempt to transform it.

After the second failure, some of the children stopped trying and began to fiddle with the objects (they would examine the box, play with it, play a game of patience with the cards, etc.), while others would stubbornly continue the magical practice, changing the cards or their position in the box, varying the loudness of their voices in pronouncing the magic words, using different gestures, etc. After many unsuccessful attempts, these children also ceased their magic acts and began to fiddle with the objects. Only a small number of children (about 10 per cent) did not attempt the transformation and either immediately began to fiddle with the objects or regarded them with indifference.

In the presence of the experimenter (third condition) all the children expressed surprise and disappointment at their failure; they acknowledged that they had tried to transform the object, but that 'nothing happened'. Many asked the experimenter to show them the right way to put the object in the box, to pronounce the words, and to perform the transformation. Interestingly, in the presence of the experimenter, only a few children (7 per cent to 23 per cent) ventured to try again, despite their explicit desire to do so following their conversation with the adult and his further clarifications (e.g. they had to say the magic words louder, put the drawings in a different position in the box); clearly, the adult's presence embarrassed the child and represented a tangible obstacle to magical practice. It is important to note that, despite disappointment and dissatisfaction with the result, only a few children (10 per cent to 17 per cent) doubted the magical properties of the box; the others continued to believe that the box was magic, and that the reason for their failures was that they had used it incorrectly or had not pronounced the words loudly enough.

The second and the third experiments basically followed the same procedure. In Experiment 2 ('Magic table') conditions were explored which could prompt a child to believe that an inanimate object could spontaneously come to life.

In the first part of the first session (verbal behaviour), the child was asked a number of questions in a casual conversation: 'Can inanimate objects come to life?'; 'Can a rhinoceros made of playdough be transformed into a living one?'; 'Why?' The purpose was to determine whether the child possessed the natural science mode of explaining phenomena, which would prohibit the coming to life of inanimate objects in everyday reality.

After this the child was told the story of 'The magic table', in which the little girl Lena was given a table with the capacity to transform play animals placed upon it into live animals. Lena did not believe this, but she nevertheless put various toys on the table. Imagine her surprise when a toy lion placed on the table suddenly began to move about before her eyes, grow, and jump from the table. It was returned to its previous state, a toy, only by waving a magic wand. Each subject was asked to retell the story and was then asked: 'Why did the lion come alive?' If the child admitted the possibility of an object's coming to life in the context of the story, he or she would be asked the following questions: 'Does this mean that inanimate objects can come to life?' 'But why, then, did you earlier say that this was not so in real life?' The answers to these questions told us whether the children differentiated on a verbal level between the sphere of the story and the sphere of everyday reality or whether they confused the two.

In the *second session* of the experiment (actual behaviour in the absence of external control), the experimenter brought the children individually into the room and showed them a little table outwardly identical with the table depicted in the illustrations of the story. The construction of the table was such that within it, under an opaque plexiglass covering, was a magnet, which, by means of a special mechanism, could be rotated noiselessly in a plane parallel to the surface of the table. The mechanism was switched on and off from another room, from which the experimenter observed the child's behaviour through an opening in a screen. The experimenter asked the child: 'Do you want me to show you the magic table from the story? Here it is!' Then he placed some playdough animal figures (a rabbit, a squirrel, a rhinoceros and a lion) beside the table. A magnet had been inserted in one of the toys (the lion); thus, if the toy was placed on the table, it would suddenly begin to move along its surface, creating the impression of having come to life. With the toys the experimenter gave the child a 'magic wand' and warned: 'If any of the animals comes to life, you can wave this wand and say "Magic, stop your work!" and it will become a toy again.' Then the experimenter, on some pretext, would leave the room and observe the child's behviour through the opening in the screen for five minutes. If the child placed the lion on the table, the experimenter would switch on the mechanism and cause the toy to move about. The rest of the strategy of the experiment depended on the children's behaviour. If they left the room, the experimenter would go in and take the toy from the table; if the children waved the magic wand, the toy would stop rotating; however, it would begin again if the children extended a hand to the toy.

We assumed that in this conflict situation the children's behaviour would demonstrate whether they possessed an *animistic interpretation* of a physical phenomenon (sudden movement of the toy along an immobile surface). If this interpretation did take place, i.e. if the children believed in the possibility of objects coming to life, in the particular situation three types of behaviour could be expected from him or her. First, the children might not place the lion and the rhinoceros on the table, restricting their handling to the 'less dangerous' animals; second, if they placed the lion on the table and saw it move, they might stop it with a wave of the magic wand; third, seeing the odd behaviour of the object, the children might leave the room. If, however, there were no animistic presumption, the children would attempt rationally to understand the phenomenon: they would calmly observe the toy rotating, try to find the mechanism that had caused it to move, etc.

At the end of the experiment the experimenter would come into the room and ask the children the causes of the phenomenon. Then the third session of experiments would be carried out, in which the experimenter would ask the children whose behaviour showed that they believed in the possibility of transforming an object to place the lion on the table; the adult would not leave the room, but observe whether the children's behaviour displayed an 'animistic presumption' in interpreting the phenomenon in the presence of external control from the experimenter.

The results of the experiment basically resembled the results of Experiment 1 (Figure 3.2).

As in the previous experiment, the children's behaviour in the real experimental situation was in striking contrast to this verbal belief of

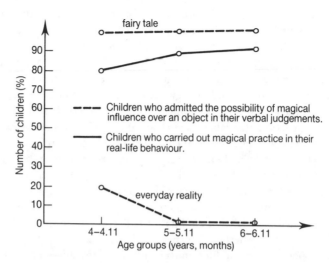

Figure 3.2 Children's behaviour in the 'Magic table' situation

theirs about the impossibility of an object coming to life. First, left alone, all the children immediately would try to bring the rabbit and squirrel to life; however, more than half of the children refused to place the figure of the lion on the table. Some of the children expressed this refusal directly, even before the experiment began ('I don't want to put the dangerous animals on the table; they might come to life after all').

With the children who refused to place the lion on the table, the experimenter proceeded as follows: after five minutes of observation, he went into the room and asked the child once more to try to bring all the toys to life; when the child placed the lion on the table, the experimenter went out of the room and switched on the apparatus.

The children could be divided into two groups according to how they accommodated to the phenomenon of a toy suddenly beginning to move. The behaviour of the children in the first group showed a distinct belief in the spontaneous coming to life of an object; but here, too, the children behaved differently. Some, seeing the toys move, quickly left the room and, meeting the experimenter outside the door, reported that the toy was 'coming to life'. Other children, seeing the toy move, would stop it with a wave of the magic wand. After the toy stopped, the child generally would observe it for a time without moving (sometimes with triumphant exclamations – 'There it is!'; 'It's magic!'; 'It's coming to life!' etc.), and then would slowly approach the object with hand extended.

Other subjects (second group) showed no signs of believing in the toy's coming to life; they would observe the toy with interest, take it in their hands, handle it, and in general accept the phenomenon as something curious, but in no way supernatural.

The post-experiment interview showed that, despite the fact that most of the children displayed similar behaviour, indicating a belief in the possibility of a transformation, they dealt with it differently at the verbal level. Most of the children said that the cause of the toy's movement was the magical qualities of the table, giving basically four different types of interpretations of what had occurred. Some children said that the lion had come to life, grown and jumped from the table, but that they had transformed it into a toy again by waving the magic wand. Others said that the toy had begun to come to life, but they had not allowed it to grow, and had stopped it. Still others said that the lion had 'come to life', but for some reason did not grow. Finally, in the fourth interpretation, the toy simply moved about, but remained inanimate; these children were unable to explain the reason for the movement and, when asked why they decided not to take the toy from the table, they would give an answer contradictory to the preceding one ('But what if he had opened his mouth?'; 'What if he would bite?'; 'I was afraid he would bite . . .'). Three children from the older age group and four of the preparatory group gave a natural science interpretation of the phenomenon ('There's a magnet inside, and it turns around . . '; 'There's some motor in the drawer . . .'; 'Because there's some mechanism in the table that moves'). Interestingly, in the real situation five of these children clearly demonstrated their belief in the possibility of animation of the object, left the room, or used the magic wand.

In Experiment 3 ('Strange Automobile') one more type of magical belief was studied, namely, whether children under certain conditions were able to acknowledge that they could set a physical object into motion with their magical manipulation and without a physical contact.

The general logic of the design of this cycle of experiments was analogous to that of the preceding one. After the child was told a story about 'The strange automobile' that had been set into motion by the story hero by saying three magic words and moving the picture with his fingers along the table, the subjects were asked questions to determine whether they admitted the possibility of the movement of an inanimate object under the influence of 'magic words' or on the strength of the movement of its picture in the sphere of everyday reality.

After a few days the child was invited into the experimental room, where a large toy automobile stood on the floor; a picture of the automobile was on a table. The experimenter said: 'Do you remember I told you about the strange automobile? Well here it is, and this is the magic picture.' Then the experimenter would recall the magic words to the child, go out of the room, and observe the child's behaviour through an opening in the screen.

It was hypothesized that if a child harboured an animistic explanation of phenomena in the background, in this particular situation it should show up in his attempts to get the automobile to move with the aid of the magic words; if, however, the children did not admit the possibility of exerting an influence on the object with words or with the picture, they would attempt to accommodate to the object rationally and would handle both the toy and its picture in ways appropriate to them (he or she would examine the toy, look at the picture, etc.).

The third session of the experiment (demonstration of an unusual phenomenon) was carried out directly after the second was finished. The experimenter would tell the children that their failure was actually due to the fact that they had not pronounced the magic words loudly enough, and would ask the children to repeat them again. He would go out of the room and then, without the children's noticing, set the automobile in motion by means of a remote control device just at the moment the children began to move the picture. After several successful attempts, the experimenter would come into the room and ask the children to explain the phenomenon.

The results (see Figure 3.3) did not substantially differ from the results of the two preceding experiments except that this time almost all the children tried to exercise magical influence upon the object. After they were shown the phenomenon almost all the children gave a 'magical' interpretation, conceding that the automobile had been moved by the magic words and the magic picture.

When asked why they had previously not admitted the possibility of a magical influence, the subjects said that they 'had been wrong', and pointed out the phenomenon they had observed as a proof that they had been wrong ('But I didn't know that you would bring the car'; 'I didn't know; I'm still little'). Some of the children admitted the possibility of magic in real life, but restricted it in space and time, saying that it was

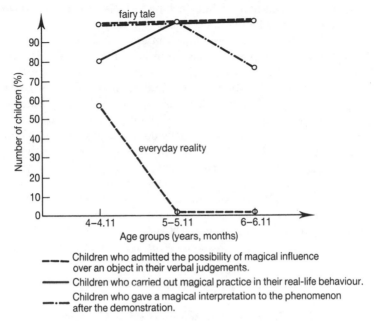

Figure 3.3 Children's behaviour in the 'Strange automobile' situation

'only sometimes' and 'only here with you and in a fairy tale, but it generally almost never happens'. Some children combined natural scientific and animistic presumptions in their explanations: on the one hand, they would say that the car moved because of natural, but unknown reasons ('from an antenna'; 'There's a motor somewhere'; 'There must be some sort of an invisible wire that moves it'), and, on the other, would say that the magical properties of the words and the picture had been the cause of the movement. Finally, four 6-year-old children emphatically rejected the possibility of a magical interpretation, although they were unable to explain the phenomenon in terms of natural causes ('I don't know what trick you use, but there's no magic here'; 'There must be a motor in it somewhere'; 'There is a wire hooked up somewhere, and that's what moved . . .').

One particular problem that arises in these experiments is why children who well know that magical causality 'doesn't work' in the domain of everyday reality readily applied it in a real, practical situation. In suggesting a solution to this problem it might be helpful to apply again the distinction between verbal and real levels of behaviour (see Chapter 1).

It may be assumed that physical causality as a concept (and not as an *intuitive action*, which may be traced even in young infants' behaviour) occurs first at the verbal, 'theoretical' level of behaviour where it exists as a legitimate, 'true' way of absorbing and understanding phenomena. The concept of magical causality, which must appear at the same time as a categorical opposition, is, however, regarded by the child as 'incorrect', as something that only 'seems', but actually does not exist within everyday reality. At the level of practical (involved) activity the existentialization may be different: the differentiation between 'faulty' and 'true' may be quite vague, and magical causality may seem to children, perhaps under influence of fairy tales, to be a much more reliable way of reaching a practical goal than through physical causality. Consequently, *even if children are taught by adults that magic 'doesn't work' in real life*, magical causality may *still keep its original dominant status* in children's practical actions.

Phenomenalistic and physical causality in the preschooler's mind: a struggle for dominance

In order to test this hypothetical model we turned not to magical but to phenomenal causality. Phenomenal causality is not psychological causality (to which magical causality belongs); nevertheless, it has the same emotional 'underpinning' as magical causality: in their phenomenal causal judgements children consider event A to be a cause of event B, not because they understand this connection in a rational way, but because this connection seems plausible to them. Since it is this type of causality and not the magical one (see Huang, 1930) that dominates in verbal judgements of 4–6-year-olds, it represents suitable material for designing an experimental model aimed at testing the role of teaching children 'a right way' to see causal connections.

In other words, I hypothesized that, at *a certain stage* in a child's acquiring scientific and rational understanding of objective relations, *there should exist a discrepancy between the orientation of verbal behaviour and that of the real (practical) level of behaviour* – i.e. at the verbal level a child will assimilate phenomena by a rational scientific method, whereas in practical actions the same phenomena will be assimilated on the basis of their phemomenal perception (unmediated by scientific conceptions).

Proving this hypothesis requires setting up experimental situations structured around objective relations (phenomena) whose phenomenal perception differs substantially from their rational scientific (or quasi-scientific) perception. In the one case the child must assess these relations at a verbal, theoretical, abstract level, and in the other, he or she must use these objective relations to achieve some practical result. If a child expresses a phenomenal perception of a phenomenon verbally, it is necessary to explain to him or her the illusoriness of this perception and to give him or her a correct, rational picture. A comparison of the rational perception, which the child has learned, with practical activity should show to what extent phenomenal perception is 'persistent' and retained in practical activity despite the child's having correctly understood a rational view of the world.

In one of the experiments designed to check this hypothesis I used the Huang procedure (see Huang, 1930), after adapting it to my purpose (Subbotsky, 1990). Three small, transparent, plastic beakers were placed before the child. One contained a weak solution of a base (NaOH); the second, a weak solution of acetic acid; and the third, a phenolphthalein solution. Outwardly all of the solutions looked no different from ordinary water. Together with the beakers were two small cardboard cylinders (red and white) equal in height to the beakers, but somewhat greater in diameter.

In the first session, the children were shown the content of all the beakers and asked what colour the water in them was. Hearing that the water was in each case 'white', the experimenter asked: 'And what colour would the water be if I poured water from this beaker (pointing to the beaker with phenolphthalein) into this beaker (the beaker with the base solution)?' While waiting for the child to answer, the adult placed the red cylinder over the beaker containing the base solution and poured the phenolphthalein solution into it. The solution turned bright red before the child's eyes. After removing the cylinder, the experimenter asked: 'What colour did the water become?' 'Why did it become red?' After hearing the answer, the adult would then ask the following question: 'And if we add this red liquid to this transparent water (pointing to the acid solution), what colour will it be?' Then, after hearing the child's response, he poured the red solution into the beaker containing the acid, after first putting a white cylinder over it. This solution again became transparent. He then took the cylinder away and repeated his questions: 'What colour did the water become?' 'Why did it become white?'

One of the purposes of this session was to determine whether the child was experiencing phenomenal perception of a cause. We assumed that, as occurred in Huang's experiments, the children would perceive the presence of the cylinder as the cause of the water's colour. They got this impression because of the spatial proximity and similarity of the cylinders in colour to the colour of the solutions, although during the experiment we gave them the possibility of discovering that the cylinders did not come into contact with the beakers containing the solutions.

In addition, we tried to give the child a rational quasi-scientific explanation of the phenomenon. Thus, at the end of the experiment, the experimenter explained 'why this actually happened'. He said: 'Look, in this beaker [the beaker with the base solution] there were small, white, invisible balls with hoops swimming around and the same kind of balls with hooks in this one (the beaker with phenolphthalein). When I poured the water from one beaker into the other, the balls came together, the hooks hooked onto hoops, and as a result they became red. But in this beaker (the beaker containing the acid solution) invisible balls with little hammers were swimming about. As soon as the red balls came near them, they would smash them with the little hammers, and the red balls would again become white.' As the story was being told, the children were shown drawings with little balls on them and what happened to them (Figure 3.4), and were asked to repeat the explanation, after which the adult said: 'And you see these little circles (he would point to the cardboard cylinders), I just placed them there; they had no influence on the colour of the little balls.' Thus, as in the preceding experiments, we attempted to make the children conscious of the two different methods of interpretation of the same phenomena: the phenomenal (the colour of water changes under the influence of the cylinders) and the rational (the colour of the water changes under the influence of the interaction of invisible balls).

About an hour after the first session was run, the subject would again be invited into the room and asked to do what was necessary for the 'water' in the one beaker to become red, and the water in the other beaker to again become white; for a reward (but only in case of success) he or she was promised a pretty postage stamp (second session). The purpose was to determine which of the two interpretations of the cause of the

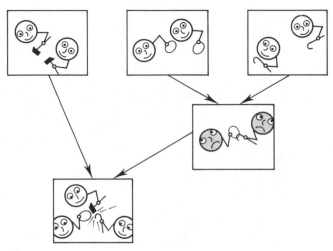

Figure 3.4 A rational explanation of the phenomenon of the solution's change of colour

phenomenon would be used by the children to guide their actions to achieve a practical result: the phenomenal (in which case they would use the cylinders) or the rational (in which case they would simply pour water from one beaker into the other).

In light of what we have said, we may doubt whether children used the cylinders because they considered them the cause of the colour of the water: perhaps they were simply imitating the actions of the adult. However, we think the term *imitation* cannot explain the cause of behaviour since it in itself requires explanation. The question is *why* children imitated a particular action of the adult, i.e. what was the *motive for imitation*. Clearly, these motives vary from one particular case to another. For example, when children copy the clothing and the manners of an adult's social behaviour, they are trying to appear adults in the eyes of other people (and in their own eyes); when they imitate the heroes of a movie, they are attempting to satisfy their own need for pretending, etc. Clearly, in the practical situation being studied here, children can imitate for only one reason: an attempt to act effectively, considering therefore the adult's action probably to be the most correct and hence entailing the greatest guarantee of success. But this means that imitation in such cases expresses the child's conscious or unconscious confidence that the presence of the cylinders is at least one, if not the only, cause of the colour of the water, i.e. it is a *mode of expression of a phenomenal perception of cause*.

In the third session we again asked the children to explain why, as a result of their actions, the water became red and then again became white. If in the second session the children used the cylinders and in the third gave a rational explanation, this would mean that phenomenal and rational perception of cause can coexist autonomously at different levels of life practice: at the level of real, practical behaviour, and at the level of verbal, theoretical behaviour.

Children from the junior (4 year olds), senior (5 year olds), and preparatory (6 year olds) groups of a kindergarten in Moscow, 20 in each, took part in the experiment. From Figure 3.5 we see that almost all the children said that the cylinders were the cause of the colour of the water. When asked why the water became red, they answered: 'Because this [pointing to the cylinder] was standing there'; 'Because this hood is red'; 'Because you placed this thing [cylinder] and there was paint there, on this paper, so the water became red too'; 'There's this paint [on the cylinder], and it passed into the water'; 'Because this paint came off the round thing.' Only three of the children in the preparatory group gave a rational explanation ('I think that there was some kind of solution in this

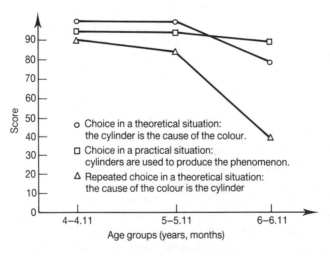

Figure 3.5 Judgement about cause in theoretical and practical situations

beaker'; 'I think that there was water here and a manganese compound here'; 'Because you poured some medicine there, and then added some soda and diluted it'). Roughly the same answers were given to the question concerning the cause of the solution's losing its colour in the acid. After hearing the experimenter's interpretation of the phenomenon, all the children satisfactorily repeated it, and also said that the cardboard cylinders had no influence on the colour of the water.

In the second session of experiments, all the subjects except four used the cylinders to produce the phenomenon. Most of the children placed a cylinder over the necessary beaker without hesitation and decanted the solution; when they saw the reaction, they could not conceal their joy ('There, it happened!' 'It changed colour!'), and then would perform the same operation with the white cylinder. Some of the children hesitated, several times, taking first the cylinder and then the beaker containing phenolphthalein. Four of the children produced the reactions without using the cylinders.

The third session showed that most of the 4- and 5-year-old children and some of the 6-year-olds lost the rational interpretation given by the experimenter and again repeated that the cause of the solution's change of colour was the cylinder ('Why did the water become red for you?' 'Because I placed the cardboard there, and it is all red, so the water became red too.' 'And why did it again become white?' 'For the same reason: it [the cylinder] is coloured white, and it absorbed quite a bit, and so it became white water'). Two of the subjects in the junior, 3 in the senior, and 12 in the preparatory group retained their rational interpretation of the phenomenon. These children, in turn, fell into three subgroups. Those who in the second session did not use the cylinder in this session gave a purely rational interpretation corresponding to the adult's explanation. The children in the second subgroup used the cylinders in the second session, but in the third session rejected their role ('Why should the water become red?' 'There are invisible little balls in it.' 'And why did you put a red hood over the beaker?' 'Because I simply did it, because . . . it doesn't mean anything.' 'And why did the water again become white?' 'That's when the little hammers smash the little balls.' 'And why did you put the white cardboard over the beaker?' 'Just so . . . it doesn't mean anything either'). Finally, the children in the third subgroup also used the cylinders in the second session, but in the third session they combined a rational interpretation with acknowledgment of the role of the 'hats' (e.g. cylinders); in their opinion, the cause of the change of colour of the water was the interaction of 'balls', but at the same time the phenomenon simply would not take place without the 'hats'. On the whole, the average number of children six years of age among those who retained a rational interpretation of the phenomenon considerably increased ($P < 0.01$). In the first and second sessions no age-related differences were observed in the subjects' behaviour.

The results seem to be quite revealing with respect to the role of verbal educational influence in changing the existential status of various forms of causality. It is obvious that any teaching (not only of preschoolers but also of schoolchildren and even adults) is more than merely communicating to a subject some knowledge filling some 'cognitive vacuum' in his or her consciousness. Usually, new knowledge will inevitably struggle with earlier, spontaneously developed forms of perception and comprehension of reality for the dominance in individual consciousness (and this includes comprehension of causal relations). But this expulsion does not take place by itself: archaic and, in particular, phenomenal forms of perception of reality create resistance.

As a result the question arises about the new existential status acquired by the archaic forms of causality (to which, no doubt, magical and phenomenal types of causality belong) once they lose their legitimate status within everyday reality of the mind.

Theoretically speaking, there might be three models of the relationships between the new and the old structures (see Figure 3.6). After being proved 'false' the old representations may vanish ('evaporate') from

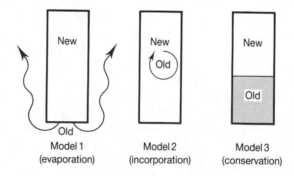

Model 1
(evaporation)

Model 2
(incorporation)

Model 3
(conservation)

Figure 3.6 Models of the interrelationships between new and old structures of the mind

the children's minds; they may be incorporated (as only partially 'true') into the new representations; or, finally, they may be conserved in their own right somewhere in children's consciousness. Obviously, with respect to the fundamental structures which exist as categorical oppositions (i.e. as magical vs. physical causality) the only relevant model is the third one.

However, even if the archaic structure is conserved in the human mind, its real existential status may vary. It can be retained, for instance, in the status of 'weak existence', as a stable illusion that has only intangible and 'ethereal' being. Quite a few examples of this type of conservation of old knowledge can be found in studies of children's ability to distinguish between 'appearance' and 'reality': as they grow older children begin to separate easily the phenomenal picture of objects from their rational constructions and arrange them in a hierarchical order (Flavel, 1986). The 'appearances' do not disappear with age, sometimes they even begin to be mentioned in judgements of older children (as a result of the vanishing of 'intellectual realism errors') and are not mentioned in judgements of younger ones; but they are being ascribed 'weak' existential status, they are not 'taken seriously'. This type of conservation is especially easy to trace in studies of verbal judgements.

If, however, *real behaviour* is taken as a subject for study, another type of conservation may be found. The 'retired' structure, even being considered as 'false', may still retain its real power and even compete with the new one. It seems likely that it is exactly this type of conservation which 'archaic' forms of causality are subject to. Interestingly enough, that in the experiment described the introduction of a rational interpretation and even the presence of an adult directly pointing out that the cylinders had nothing to do with the effect observed not only did not destroy the actuality of a phenomenal cause but even itself proved unstable. An absolute majority of the children were oriented towards a phenomenal cause of the phenomenon in their practical actions, and when a 'theoretical' explanation was repeated, 4–5-year-old subjects (with the exception of five children) and about half the 6-year-olds returned to the phenomenal interpretation. Thus, the phenomenal perception of causality was stable in these children and regarded as the 'only correct' one in their practical actions and in their verbal judgements.

The stability of phenomenal perception continued to be high in children of the oldest age group (6-year-olds): 90 per cent of them were guided by it in their practical actions, and in the third session, 70 per cent of the children regarded the cylinders as either the only cause or one of the causes of the change in the water's colour. But at this age, the stability of a rational explanation increased considerably: it was retained by 60 per cent of the subjects. Nevertheless, half of them combined a rational explanation with a phenomenal explanation; we found a 'clear' discrepancy between the phenomenal and rational perceptions of cause in only 4 (20 per cent) of the subjects of this age (they used the cylinders in the second session and denied their role in the third session). However, for a very small number of children (7 per cent of the total number of subjects), introduction of a rational interpretation destroyed the phenomenal interpretation both 'in theory' and 'in practice'.

How can we explain these experimental results? It may be assumed that the relationship between the two types of perception of causal relations depends essentially on their 'psychological (or existential) weight' in the children's consciousness. For phenomenal perception this 'weight' depends on the emotional significance and distinctness of the impression produced. Hence, it is quite likely that if the obviousness and the distinctness of the phenomenon is less marked, the phenomenon cannot compete with the new knowledge and simply disappears from the children's minds (as it was shown with respect to one of Piaget's phenomena in the same study: Subbotsky, 1990).

As for rational perception, its 'psychological weight' depends on the level of children's knowledge and their capacity to operate freely with the instruments mediating the objective relations they perceive. It may be assumed that the relationship between these two factors determines the status of archaic mental structures, causality included. The low 'weight' of a phenomenal structure and the substantial 'weight' of a new 'scientific' structure destroys the phenomenal structure and completely supplants it with the scientific one both at the level of verbal judgement and at the level of practical actions. The inverse relationship may be expected to produce the opposite result.

With regard to causality, the phenomenal 'pressure' of the apparent causal connections, based both upon spatial proximity and colour resemblance, must have been relatively strong. On the other hand, the 'quasi-scientific' explanation given to the children was still extremely complicated, abstract and too elusive for them to operate with independently. Consequently, it had little 'psychological weight'. As a result, the psychologically strong phenomenal perception blocked out the influence of the psychologically weak rational explanation on the child's actual behaviour and quickly eliminated this explanation from the sphere of verbal judgements.

However, in a small number of subjects in the older age group (six years of age) both types of causal explanation coexisted. It means that a certain dynamic equilibrium between the psychological weight of phenomenal perception and that of rational perception was achieved in the children's minds. The rational physical causality governed at the level of the children's verbal judgements in a 'theoretical' situation, while phenomenal causality continued to rule the children's practical actions. The same dynamic equilibrium was observed with respect to a visual illusion (Subbotsky, 1990). Similar equilibrium may have occurred in the relationship between physical and magical causality notions in the minds of most preschoolers. The discrepancy between verbal and real behaviour in the 'magic box' experiment was so widely spread that it was reasonable to view it as a typical characteristic of preschool age. This prompted us to continue the study with older subjects.

Studies with older children and adults

Obviously, a dynamic equilibrium of this type cannot be very stable and may be shifted in both directions. As children's intellectual capacities expand, the influence of culture can grow as well. As a result, the 'existential weight' of magical or physical causality in children's minds may gain in strength and force the opposite structure out of the sphere of everyday reality. Whereas in certain 'traditional' cultures magical causality may occupy a legitimate status in the everyday reality of adults (see, for instance, Mead, 1932), in European cultures we might expect the opposite to be true. It may be assumed, therefore, that at older ages European children will be more apt to assimilate the above-described phenomena relying on the physical causality. In order to test this hypothesis, the 'magic box' experiment was conducted with pupils from grades 1, 2 and 3 (31, 30 and 29 students respectively).* The results are shown in Figure 3.7.

---

* The experiments were conducted in Moscow by S. V. Girnis in his diploma project (Girnis, 1985).

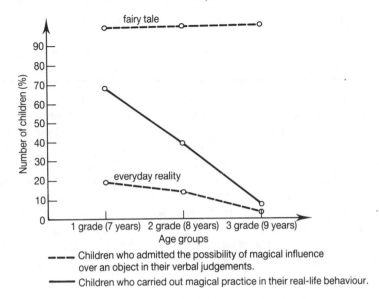

Figure 3.7 Children's behaviour in the 'Magic box' situation (school age)

A comparison of the results with those given by the preschoolers (see Figure 3.1) showed no significant differences between the preschoolers and the 1st graders. However, children from the 2nd and 3rd grades used the magical mode of assimilation of phenomenon in their real behaviour far less frequently than the preschool children. It also emerged that the use by the children of the physical or magical causality at the level of real behaviour in the experiment did not correlate with the children's results at school ($r = -0.04$ for the pupils of the 1st grade and $r = 0.25$ for the pupils of the 2nd grade).

On the whole, these data confirmed the assumption that the effectiveness of magical causality within the sphere of everyday reality in the older children tended to decrease; although at the level of the verbal (non-involved) assimilation of the phenomenon the conduct of the children did not actually change (i.e. the magical causality is practically excluded by the children from the sphere of everyday reality), at the level of real behaviour the schoolchildren applied the magical practice far more rarely than the preschool age children. The most vivid manifestation of this tendency was found in the pupils of the third grade, almost none of whom applied magical practice.

This age tendency can hardly be explained by the fact that the notion of the magical causality vanishes from the child's consciousness. Rather, these data merely reveal the process of differentiation between the domains of everyday and unusual realities and the strengthening of the border that separates them. This differentiation having been achieved at the preschool age at the level of verbal behaviour, it stays relatively unstable at the level of practical actions until the child reaches the 3rd grade. The absence of a significant correlation between children's achievements at school and their tendency to apply magical causality in the 'Magic box' experiment testifies against the direct influence of school education on the differentiation between various domains of reality.

The strengthening of the border between realities, however, does not mean that magical causality disappears from adults' minds. Taking for granted that it continues to exist legitimately within unusual realities of the mind, it might be assumed that, under certain conditions, it is reactivated even in everyday practice. Such conditions may emerge, for instance, in a state of frustration, occurring as a result of the impossibility of solving a problem relying on natural causality: one might expect that in such a state the boundary between the domains of everyday and unusual realities would weaken and the adult subject would be more apt to apply to magical causality.

To verify this hypothesis it was necessary to confront adult subjects with an insoluble problem in such a way that their awareness of the fact that the problem could not be solved by ordinary means would emerge gradually (i.e., at first the task must seem to the subject to be a soluble one). As the subject enters into a stage of frustration, he or she is offered an attempt to solve the problem by magical means. If the hypothesis is correct, then with growing frustration the subject should be more willing to turn to magical means that had previously seemed impossible.

In this experiment* the method elaborated by T. Dembo was used (see Levin, 1935). The experimenter drew a square with a piece of chalk in the corner of the room (2×2 m). From the external side of the square a vase with a flower in it was put on a table at a distance inaccessible for

---

* The experiment was conducted in Moscow by A. P. Grivtsov in his student's research project (Grivtsov, 1988).

individuals to reach with their hands when standing inside the square. A chair was placed beside the square. The problem was presented to the subjects as a test of intelligence and creative thinking: 'It is necessary to get the flower without stepping out of the square.' The subjects quickly arrived at the only two possible ways of getting the flower (to lie on the floor leaving their feet inside the square or to get the flower leaning their arms on the chair).

Having approved the subjects' actions, the experimenter told them that there might still be another way of tackling the task. A minute or two later, when the subjects realized the difficulty of the task, the experimenter asked them: 'And what do you think about telekinesis? Do you think that if you mentally concentrate upon the flower and try to feel its approach with your palms like that you can take the flower after all? Would you like to try?' Irrespective of the answer, the experimenter told the subjects that it was highly desirable to take the flower by means of another method. If in the course of 40 minutes the subjects did not turn to the telekinesis (which in this case was a culturally acceptable form of the magical influence upon the object) then the experiment was over and the true purpose of the experiment was revealed to the subjects.

Twenty-three subjects (age range 16 to 34 years) took part in the experiment. As a result, none of the subjects tried to influence the object through 'telekinesis' immediately. Listening attentively to the experimenter's explanations, they persisted in their attempts to find another natural-causal solution to the task. As time passed, the subjects developed a growing emotional tension. At the end of the experiment all of the subjects came to the conclusion that telekinesis was the only real method of solving the task, although only four of them tried it.

In sum, the data showed that magical causality could be reactivated in the consciousness of adult subjects to an extent that it started to exercise an influence on their practical actions. However, this release cannot be achieved except by great efforts and in conditions of strong emotional tension. Although the adults readily applied to magical causality (which in order to be acceptable to speak of, should have been 'wrapped' in the pseudoscientific terminology) in their fantasies, most of them did not try to use it in practice. Partially, however, it may be accounted for by the constant presence of the experimenter: it was quite obvious that the subjects were shy of applying magic, and they might have been much less reluctant in doing so had they been left alone.

Conclusions

Thus, the experiments showed that, in the sphere of everyday reality, two opposite types of assimilation of phenomena actually exist in a child. At the *verbal level*, a natural scientific presumption in explanations clearly predominates even in five-year-olds. This predominance may be interpreted in terms of the specificity of this behavioural level.

Essentially, this specificity consists in the fact that it ensures the most favourable possibilities for the manifestation (existence) of *legitimate norms*. On the one hand, verbal behaviour takes place in a situation of direct control (conversations with an adult), which makes the use of socially approved (in this particular case, natural scientific) norms for assimilating reality advantageous for the child. On the other hand, the use of contrast (animistic) norms in this situation is totally unmotivated, or motivated only negatively (fear of being judged by the interviewer). No wonder, therefore, that the natural scientific mode of explanation predominated in the sphere of everyday reality at the verbal level; however, in the realm of a fairy tale, in which the contrasting animistic method of explanation is also approved socially, all the children unanimously admitted the possibility of extraordinary phenomena.

There was one other peculiarity of the natural scientific explanation that was characteristic of five-year-olds – a blurred line between the fairy-tale world and real life at the level of a verbal discussion. Thus, after hearing a story, a considerable number of the children in the middle and older age groups changed their opinion and admitted the possibility of extraordinary phenomena in the sphere of everyday life as well; only the six-year-olds were able to draw a sharp line between the world of fairy tale and everyday life, between the possible and the impossible, and between the natural and the supernatural at the level of verbal behaviour.

Finally, we should emphasize the *instability* of natural scientific explanations of phenomena at the level of everyday reality: most of the children made use of such explanations only in an abstract situation, but after they had observed an extraordinary phenomenon, they had recourse to a magical mode of explanation.

An analysis of the *real-life behaviour* of the children in the absence of external control produced another picture. We found that even in the sphere of everyday reality, an animistic presumption for explaining phenomena predominated totally and fully: the behaviour of most of the children in all three experiments directly demonstrated their belief in the possibility of spontaneous transformation of an object and of exerting a magic influence on an object. Once again we saw the reasons for this as lying in the specific features of the motivational structure of real-life behaviour, which create favourable conditions for the manifestation of contrasting animistic norms.

On the one hand, the application of these norms in the given situation is quite *positively motivated* (the endeavour to get an attractive object, to move the automobile, fear of an animal that has come to life); on the other hand, there was no negative motivation of animistic norms in the form of external control by an adult. As for natural scientific norms for explaining phenomena, in this particular situation, the application of these norms by the child was reinforced by a cognitive motive alone, since external control was absent. This resulted in the finding that in this particular situation, an animistic presumption for explaining the world predominated for the children in the sphere of everyday reality. However, this presumption again gave way to natural cause-and-effect explanations as soon as the external control of an adult was again introduced.

The child's observation of an unusual phenomenon not only 'released' an animistic presumption for explaining the world at the level of real-life behaviour but also substantially distorted the child's verbal behaviour. Here, too, the line between the possible and the impossible, the natural and the supernatural, fluctuated even among the older preschool children. An absolute majority of the children acknowledged the possibility that the 'magical' existed in everyday reality, and only a few gave a natural scientific interpretation. Some of the children characteristically attempted to restrict an unusual phenomenon in time and space (a magical phenomenon is possible, but only 'sometimes' and only 'here with you'); in this way a child attempted to preserve the integrity of his or her natural scientific picture of the world by isolating some 'rupture' that had taken place in it.

Thus, the genesis of two opposite modes of explaining the world appear to us not to take place *successively*, one after the other (which is neither theoretically not practically possible), but as a simultaneous movement in a two-dimensional 'psychological space'. On the one hand, this movement takes place on the two different levels of behaviour (verbal and real). On the other hand, this movement takes place in different spheres of the child's life practice: hence, an animistic presumption assumes the predominant (legitimate) position in the sphere of the fairy tale, fantasy and art, whereas in everyday reality, norms of a natural scientific picture of the world become legitimate; as for animistic norms, in everyday reality they are pushed into the background, although they do not lose their fundamental psychological significance.

This competition for dominance between two opposite modes of causality may be quite complex and lead to temporary 'gains' and 'losses' on both sides. The final result may depend on the relative psychological 'weight' of archaic (phenomenalistic and magical) and scientific (physical) causality in children's minds, which in its own right may depend upon a number of factors, from purely 'perceptive' (spatial proximity, colour, etc.), to cultural (a predominance of a certain causality mode in a given culture).

The distinct age patterns in the two ways of explaining the world that we noticed in the sphere of everyday reality in our experiments (a decrease in the importance of a magical explanation among the older children) corresponds completely to their relative weight in an adult reared within European culture (with an overwhelming predominance of a natural scientific mode of explaining phenomena). This pattern may be explained by the influence of two factors: on the one hand, the external social control over a child's behaviour intensifies with age and helps to suppress magical practice; on the other hand, the domain of application of the instrument of a rational scientific mode of explaining phenomena becomes wider (knowledge, abilities, skills). Nevertheless, both our findings and our observations indicate that there is some irreducible 'vestige' in the psychological life of an adult that is outside the control of rational scientific instruments and leaves a 'vital space' for the appearance of the practice of magic.

Thus, the dynamic relationship between physical and magical causality in the mind of the individual basically looks very similar to that between permanence and nonpermanence in physical objects. It is now the time to see whether the development of two other fundamental structures – space and time – follows the same model.

Chapter 4

The development of the notions of space and time in a child

The concept of space contains a certain element of indefiniteness. As distinct from an object, which is in its essence a quite definite 'clot of being', space (like time) is a pure form, in which the objects of the outer world are given to us, and therefore can be described but indirectly through the description of objects and their relations. One should differentiate the fundamental properties (structures) underlying notions of space and time from the properties traditionally investigated (metrical and topological object relations with regard to space, measurement of time periods through movement and other simple processes with regard to time).

The fundamental structure that underlies the idea of space is the opposition between permeability and impermeability of one physical body with respect to another and its variants (the opposition of soft–solid, empty–full, etc.). It is just this opposition of categories that was a framework for early concepts of the structure of the universe, such as Democritus' and Epicurus' concepts of atoms and vacuum, Diodor Kron's idea of invisible particles, and so on (see Sextus Empiricus, 1976). This opposition is also present in contemporary metatheories of physical space: the classical 'empty space' of Isaac Newton and nonclassical 'space of edges and surfaces' proposed by James Gibson are both inconceivable without the opposition of empty and full, permeable and impermeable, and borders that separate them.

With regard to time, an equally fundamental structure is the reversibility–irreversibility of complex processes. In contrast to the world of Newton's classical dynamics – the world of eternal and unchangeable natural laws which exist, in fact, beyond time – modern science deals with irreversible processes (see Prigogine and Stengers, 1986). The irreversibility of existence, so strongly emphasized by ancient dialectics, is an essential feature not only of physical time, but of 'psychological time' as well.

Two positions may be detected in children's acquisition of these structures. According to one of them the process is viewed as stage-based. At birth children possess none of these structures; later on, as their experience grows, they acquire one of the poles and ascribe permeability and reversibility to all objects and processes. Step by step the opposite poles are acknowledged as well (impermeability and irreversibility); the latter are then accepted as fundamental legitimate characteristics attributed to objects and processes of the external physical world.

Obviously, this position is very close to the 'replacement model'. No wonder, therefore, that it can be easily traced in Piaget's descriptions of the development of the 'spatiotemporal' field. Although with respect to space and time the scheme of 'progressive stages' is applied not as purposefully as with respect to object and causality, it is quite detectable.

Thus, according to Piaget (1937a), subjective space, typical of the first two stages of intellectual development (from 0 to 3–4 months) is modally specific. It is a system of pictures in which children distinguish separate forms, sizes, sounds, odours, etc. Thus, within the space of the mouth ('buccal space'), children in the first months of life are capable of co-ordinating the sensorimotor schemes of the mouth and hand, of the head and eyes, accommodate the visual apparatus to the perception of objects, etc. However, all these abilities are of an automatic nature and exist only in action.

At the third stage of the development of the sensorimotor intellect (approximately 3–4 to 7–9 months) there is a co-ordination of previously independent spaces – tactile and visual, visual and buccal, tactile and audial, etc. None the less, a thorough study shows that children still lack the capability of perceiving object permanence and perceiving movement as the replacement of the object against the background of the other ones. This kind of space Piaget termed a soliptic space.

The main achievement of the fourth stage (8–12 months) is children's ability to search for an object hidden in their presence behind a screen; as this object had not been previously involved in the children's activity, their search means that they attribute permanence of existence to the object. This also points to the emergence in children of the ability (1) to perceive movement as the alteration of the position (but not the state, i.e. being) of the object in respect to other objects (e.g. in respect to the screen), and (2) to perceive the depth planes (the relations 'in front of' and 'behind'). One more aspect children acquire at this stage is the constancy of shape and size. However this space, outwardly looking like the objective and universal, in actual fact is still centred in the child. The evidence for this Piaget found in AB error, as well as in the loss by an object of its identity for the child as soon as this object spatially intersected with a larger object.

Last, at the fifth stage (12–20 months), one can see the development in children of an intuitive understanding of objective space as a sort of universal tank, in which they are situated. The criterion for such an understanding of space is the fact that children's bodies lose their roles of privileged centres, of the universal starting point; these roles are now taken by the objects surrounding them (the room, the house, the neighbourhood). Accordingly, children develop the ability to compensate for the replacement of objects within the space through various replacements of their bodies.

It is curious that, even in the fifth stage, children still lack the ability to attribute impermeability to solid objects (for instance, they make attempts to push a ring through a wooden stick as if wood were permeable). Step by step, however, the attribution of solidity and impermeability to stable physical bodies is acquired and is no longer violated.

Similarly, Piaget described the process of the development of the 'temporal field'. In the first and the second stages of sensorimotor development, children lack sensitivity to temporal characteristics since they are unable to detect a sequence of events (Piaget, 1937a). 'Before' and 'after' do not yet exist for them. During stage 3 (3–7 months) the belief in reversibility dominates in children's behaviour: infants try to reproduce interesting events through 'magical actions'. However, it is precisely in this stage that initial understanding of irreversibility appears for the first time (the so-called 'secondary secular reaction', for instance, is the ability to perceive a temporal succession of events: 'pull the string – there'll come a sound'). Later on (stages 5 and 6) children attribute irreversibility to processes more and more; they do not mix a cause and a consequence any more, the initial forms of memories and plans for the future appear.

It follows, therefore, from this description that the process of acquisition of these oppositional structures by a child is based on the 'replacement model': the child initially lacks any conception of solid (impermeable) bodies. Eventually, the infant's conceptions of subjective space and reversible subjective time are transformed (by approximately two years of age) into space and time based upon solid objects and irreversible processes.

Contrary to this view, it is possible not to consider the process as a gradual substitution of one fundamental structure by another. The ideas of impermeable object and irreversible process may be viewed as present in the child's mind from the very beginning. They coexist with the opposite ideas of permeable object and reversible process for the whole lifespan, but their domains of influence are different. In the domain of everyday reality, notions of space and time are based on the structures of mutual impermeability of solid objects and irreversibility of complex processes (physical space and time). By contrast, in the domain of unusual reality, (fairy tales, dreams, fantasies) unusual properties of space and time are attributed a legitimate status: the mutual permeability of solid objects, and the reversibility of complex processes are not ruled out.

Once this hypothesis is accepted, it is reasonable to look for these opposing fundamental structures in two directions. On the one hand, it is possible to look for early forms of the child's sensitivity to the impermeability of solid objects (or its substitutes) even during infancy, e.g. at an age when the infant, according to the traditional view, lacks this sensitivity. On the other hand, one can also expect to find the idea of a 'permeable solid object' working in the consciousness of a preschool child (or an older child) even in the domain of everyday reality.

It is just this hypothesis, albeit not explicitly stated, that seems to inspire the intensive and successful efforts to find forms of behaviour in young infants that can be interpreted as signs of a sensitivity to the mutual impermeability of solid objects and to the irreversibility of certain processes, or as prerequisites for such a sensitivity. Thus, with regard to space, these studies have shown that infants even in their first weeks of life can distinguish contours (Powers and Dobson, 1982), certain colours (Hamer, Alexander and Teller, 1982) and the main 'canonical' figures – an arrow, a triangle and a cross (Slater, Morison and Rose, 1982; for a more thorough review of early spatial abilities see Bremner, 1991). There is also evidence of early sensitivity to intermodal (possibly amodal) permeability vs. impermeability.

Thus, in studies by Gibson *et al.* (1979) and Walker *et al.* (1980) infants of three months were shown the objects performing either rigid (circulation around one of the three axes – a vertical, a horizontal and a frontal one – without altering the form as the interrelationship of components) or elastic (the object was first deformed and then restored to its former shape) movements. Through the habituation–dishabituation method the authors discovered that children of this age are capable of distinction (1) between elastic and rigid movements (irrespective of the type of movements given in the test on adaptation); (2) between various shapes of the objects given in the process of rigid movement (rotation around the axis).

From this the authors draw their principal conclusion, based on the theory of 'direct perception' (Gibson, 1979): the child can directly perceive the consistency (rigidity and elasticity) and is able to detect and adequately utilize the visual information about consistency from the peculiarities of the object's movement. (One should bear in mind, however, that they are speaking not of a displacement of one object with respect to another one, but only of a deformation and rotation of the object around its own axis.)

In another study (Gibson and Walker, 1984) babies as young as one month were habituated to two small cylinders similar in shape and size and surface but different in consistency (one was solid, and the other one was elastic). Although the adaptation had been achieved without the participation of vision (through manipulation with the objects placed in the child's mouth), the infants looked more persistently at the new objects when shown the two objects performing either rigid or elastic movements in a preference test. Similar results were achieved in experiments with 12-month-old infants who had been subjected to either purely tactile or tactile and visual acquaintance with rigid and elastic objects. The authors interpret the results of the experiments as evidence in favour of the availability in children of the a priori intermodal perception of consistency.

Although a thorough review is not my purpose, it is important to stress that the existence of the intermodal transference (and, therefore, evidence in favour of existence of a certain 'amodal space' in infants with the first year of life) has been found in a number of studies (Soroka *et al.*, 1979; Gottfried and Rose, 1980; Wagner *et al.*, 1981; Starkey *et al.*, 1983). The existence of such a 'space' would be crucial evidence in favour of the hypothesis according to which the fundamental characteristic of space (the distinction between 'permeability–impermeability') pertains not only to the tactile modality, but is a universal quality. At the moment, however, there are only a few studies showing the existence of an early ability to visually distinguish between entities permeable and impermeable for a solid object. Bower (1971) showed that babies at the age of four months express surprise at the attempt to touch an illusory cube; at the same time, touching a real tangible cube does not give rise to such a reaction; the author assumes that human beings possess a certain primitive unity of feelings (sensations), including visual variables specifying tactile consequences; and this primitive unity is built into the structure of the nervous system. Another study available is the experiment conducted by Baillargeon (1987), who demonstrated that some 3½-month-old infants expressed surprise when they saw a solid impermeable screen go through the solid body hidden behind it and were indifferent when the screen moved in a similar way in 'emptiness'.

The infants' sensitivity to the irreversibility of time has been investigated much less often. Most of the studies rely on works by Piaget and are devoted to more particular properties of time – notions of duration and sequence and their relationship to physical objects (Levin *et al.*, 1978; Levin, 1979; Goods, 1982; Levin and Gilat, 1983; Montangero, 1984).

However, there are data revealing such a sensitivity. Thus, Leslie (1986), in a series of ingenious studies, has demonstrated that 3–6-month-old infants attribute causality to particular successive events, with the implication, therefore, that the events are seen as an irreversible succession of cause and consequence.

A movement of scholars 'down the age-scale' is represented by a vast range of studies, but the counter-movement 'up the age-scale' is hardly detectable. A possible exception is studies in 'anomalistic psychology' showing the presence of 'magical thinking' (in the form of the so-called 'beliefs in the paranormal') in the mind of an adult (see Zusne and Jones, (1982). As for children of preschool and school ages, their belief in magic and animism, with a few exceptions (Harris *et al.*, 1991; Subbotsky, 1985) has been studied only in the Piagetian 'verbal' tradition, which does not permit an assessment of whether the fundamental oppositional structures (nonpermanent object, magical causality, permeable solid object, reversible time) are able to control the children's behaviour in a real, practical situation.

The experimental study of understanding of certain fundamental structures of space and time in preschoolers

In an attempt partially to remedy this gap, two experiments were undertaken in order to determine (1) whether preschool children can attribute the fundamental oppositional structures of space and time to different domains (everyday versus unusual reality); and (2) whether the unusual properties of space and time can enter the domain of everyday reality (Subbotsky, 1992).

In Experiment 1 (space) 4-, 5- and 6-year-old children participated as subjects (16, 19 and 10 children respectively).

A wooden box 27 × 40 × 22 cm with two opposite walls made of glass was employed in the experiment. The box had no lid or openings in it, so it was not possible to remove any of the objects which it contained (a fountain pen, a brooch, a ring, a cigarette lighter, a postage stamp, etc.)

Subjects were tested individually. Children in the experimental group were tested in three successive stages. In the first stage, they were asked questions about the permeability of various objects. The child was asked (1) Can you go through this wall (the wall of the room was indicated)? Why/Why not? Can it be done in a fairy tale? (2) If you see a toy behind the glass, can you stretch your hand through the glass and pick up the toy? Why/Why not? Is it possible to do that in a fairy tale? (3) If a coin is lying on the bottom of a bucket filled with water, can you pick up the coin? What is it you have to stretch your hand through to pick up the coin? Why is it possible to stretch your hand through water and imposs- ible through glass? (4) Please, take my fountain pen (the experimenter is holding the pen in his hand). What is it you've stretched your hand through in order to take the pen? What is it between your hand and the pen?

Children were then told a fairy tale about a girl who was given a 'magic box' made of glass as a present; the box contained a number of attractive objects (a fountain pen, a ring, etc.). The box could not be opened in the normal way, but if one said the 'magic words' (alpha, beta, gamma), the walls of glass became 'just like air' and one could stretch a hand through and take the objects. Children were asked to retell the story and then asked: Why has Ol'ia (the name of the story character) managed to get the ring? In real life, is it possible to make the glass 'just like air' by using magic words? The aim of these questions was to determine whether the child's belief in the impermeability of solid objects in real life could be influenced by a fairy tale.

The second stage of the experiment took place a day later. Children were given a real box similar to the box described in the story and told: 'Maybe it is a magic box as well.' Children were then reminded of the 'magic words' and told: 'You can try if you want. If you manage to get

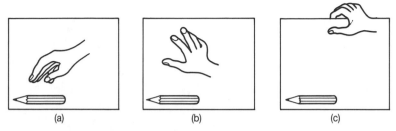

Figure 4.1 Trials with a manual posture appropriate for grasping (a), investigation (b) and practical attempts to uncover the box (c)

something out of the box, you can keep it.' The child was then left alone in the room and observed. Indices of the child's belief in the permeability of a solid object (the glass wall of the box) were judged to be those actions, that (1) occurred after the child had said the magic words, and (2) included an appropriate manual posture for grasping an object. These *magical* actions were distinguished from *investigative* actions (patting, touching, investigation of the box with a hand) and *practical* actions (attempts to open the box in an ordinary way (see Figure 4.1).

In the third stage, the experimenter returned and carried out a post-experimental interview in order to determine the child's emotional attitude towards their failure to penetrate the glass. The experimenter asked the child (1) Did you try? (2) Did you manage to get something out of the box? (3) Do you think that this box is a magical one or is it just an ordinary wooden box? If children really believed in the permeability of the glass while making grasping actions, it was expected that they would be disappointed with their failure and would reveal their disappointment in their answers to questions 1 and 2: they would complain that the magical words were not effective and ask the experimenter to show them how to act on the box properly in order for the 'magic words' to have an effect. If, however, children were simply playing a game of pretend, they would not have anticipated being able to reach the objects in the box, and, therefore, could not be expected to show disappointment (i.e. they would not complain, or request a demonstration of the proper way to penetrate the glass).

Children in the control group were simply shown the box and left alone, having been promised that anything that they could extract from the box would be given to them as a reward.

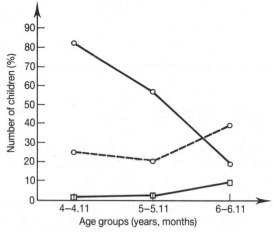

Number of children who tried to get through the glass in a magical way:
  ○—○ Experimental group.
  □—□ Control group.
  ○--○ Number of children who denied that the box was 'magical'
         at the end of the experiment.

Figure 4.2 Scores obtained in Experiment 1 (space)

The results showed that in the first stage, all subjects in the experimental groups acknowledged the impermeability of the glass and the wall for a hand in everyday reality and acknowledged the possibility of permeability in a fairy story (see Figure 4.2).

In the second stage, most of the 4- and 5-year-olds and some of the 6-year-olds tried to pass their hands through the glass as though it were permeable. The number of children who tried (at least once) to say the 'magic words' and to stretch their hands through the glass was significantly lower among 6-year-olds than among 4-year-olds ($t = 3.02$, $p < 0.02$). Most of these children clearly expressed their disappointment with the failure in the post-experimental interview (third stage). By contrast, in the control groups, only one child tried to obtain objects 'in a magical way' having made a special 'magical gesture' over the box. The rest either tried to obtain objects in a normal way or did not try at all.

Despite the fact that not all the children tried to obtain the objects in a magical way and all who tried failed, the majority of the subjects in all age groups at the end of the experiment still acknowledged that the box was 'magical'.

In Experiment 2 (time) children from the same age groups (fifteen children in each) participated as subjects. A small wooden box 15 × 11 × 11 cm was used. It had a special mechanism inside which could make a new postage stamp appear to replace a old one placed in the box (for a detailed description, see Chapter 2, Figure 2.1). In addition, there was a bottle with pure boiled water, a small box with sugar powder, an old (torn and crumpled) postage stamp, and an empty glass.

The children were tested individually. In the first stage children were asked (1) Who are you: a girl (a boy), a woman (a man) or an old woman (an old man)? (2) And who is your mother (who is your father)? (3) Who will you be when you become grown up? (4) Can your mother (your father) become a little girl (a little boy) again? Why/Why not? Is it possible in a fairy tale? (5) Can an old and damaged object turn into a new one? Why/Why not? Is it possible in a fairy tale? The aim of these questions was to assess whether children understood the irreversibility of complex processes in real life (in this case, the impossibility for a human being to become younger or for an old object to become a new one) and whether they admitted reversibility of such processes in a fairy tale.

Next, children were told a fairy tale about a girl who had been given a bottle of 'magic water', a small portion of which could 'turn you and everything around you into what it was two years ago'. At first, the story continued, the girl did not believe it, but when she tried the water (in order to bring her beloved dog back to life) she did, in fact, become a 3-year-old child. Each subject was asked to recall the story and was then asked (1) Does it mean that it is possible in real life as well, to turn time backwards? (2) But why did Lena (the heroine) become a few years younger? The aim of these questions was to determine whether the fairy tale would have any influence on the children's belief in the irreversibility of complex processes in real life.

In the second stage, the child was shown a bottle with pure boiled water, a small box with sugar powder, an old (torn and crumpled) postage stamp, and a wooden box with a special mechanism inside that could turn an old postage stamp into a new one.

The child was told that once the powder was dissolved in the water, it became 'magic' water. Children were then shown that an old postage stamp 'really' turned into a new one if it was touched by a drop of magic water (in reality, because of the mechanism concealed in the box). 'If you drink a little bit, you will probably turn into a little boy (girl),' the experimenter said, and then suggested: 'Now you can try the water, if

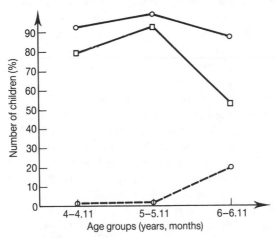

Number of children who refused to drink water:

o——o After the first request.
□——□ After the second request.
o——o Number of children who acknowledged that water was not magical at the end of the experiment.

Figure 4.3 Scores obtained in Experiment 2 (time)

you want. I just want to see if it works. But if you do not want to try – it is up to you.' If the child refused to try, the request was repeated with the promise of a postage stamp as a reward (stage 3). In order to determine whether the child's verbal disbelief in the reversibility of a complex processes in everyday reality was influenced by the experimental manipulations, the child was asked the last question: 'Now, what do you think – is this water magic or is it just ordinary sugar water?'

In the control groups, children were simply asked to try some 'sugar water' in order to find out if it was tasty.

The results of Experiment 2 are shown in Figure 4.3. Among the 4-year-olds, 33 per cent acknowledged at least one of the three possible variants of reversibility (that their mother or father or they themselves could become a little child again, or that the old object could become a new one again). The rest of the subjects were surprisingly consistent in their emphatic denial of each possible reversal ('Life does not go back', 'Time only goes ahead').

Despite the fact that all the children admitted that time-reversal could happen in a fairy tale, only three 4-year-olds and two 5-year-olds recognized the possibility of reversal in real life after they had been told the fairy tale.

In a real situation (stage 2), all the children acknowledged that the old postage stamp 'became newer' under the influence of the 'magic' water; most subjects in each age group refused to try the water following the experimenter's initial request. Most of them justified their refusal by saying that they did not want to become a little child again. When the children were promised a reward (third stage), the majority of 4- and 5-year-olds still refused the experimenter's request, but almost half of the 6-year-olds agreed. Among the 6-year-olds the total number of the children refusing to try the water was significantly lower than among the 4- and 5-year-old children combined ($t = 2.8$, $p < 0.025$). All children with the exception of three 6-year-olds answered the last question in the positive, acknowledging the water to be magic. None of the control children refused to taste some sugar water.

Conclusions

As shown in previous studies (Subbotsky, 1985, 1990), preschool children are able to differentiate verbally between what can happen in everyday reality vs. unusual realities (dreams, fairy tales, fantasy). They attribute object permanence and physical causality to the former and allow for object non-permanence and magical causality in the latter. The results of the present study reveal that children of preschool age are also able to differentiate fundamental properties of space and time in their verbal judgements: they attribute impermeability of solid objects and irreversibility of complex processes to the domain of everyday reality while admitting the opposite properties (permeability of solid objects and reversibility of complex processes) to be possible in fairy tales. However, this differentiation is not yet firm either at the level of verbal judgements or at the level of practical behaviour: it can be violated under the influence of a fairy tale and an adult's instruction. The majority of 4- and 5-year-olds and some 6-year-olds tried to pass their hand through a glass wall (in order to obtain an attractive object) and refused to drink 'magic' water (fearing to become a toddler again), thereby revealing their belief in the unusual properties of space and time in everyday reality.

As shown by the results, the differentiation between the dominant properties of space and time in everyday reality as compared with unusual realities at a verbal level was not influenced significantly by the fairy tale alone. (This did occur with causality in our previous study; Subbotsky, 1985.) However, the experimenter's instruction and manipulations with the box and water did influence children's verbal convictions: at the end of the experiment most of the children acknowledged that the box and the water were 'magic'. This means that the experimenter's credulity towards unusual phenomena is the crucial factor in changing the children's beliefs.

The fact that these changes, at least at the level of practical behaviour, were not due to simple compliance with the experimenter was guaranteed by the non-directive character of the experimenter's instruction. Indeed, in Experiment 1 the child was left alone in the room during the testing procedure, and was therefore free to decide whether or not to try to pass his or her hand through the glass; in Experiment 2, the child's autonomy was shown by the fact that the majority of the children refused the experimenter's request to try the water, thereby revealing their belief in the water's magic power. The initial reluctance of 6-year-olds to engage in a magical practice and their readiness to try the water for the reward may be interpreted as a sign of their growing conviction that in everyday reality 'normal' physical space and time predominate.

The last issue to consider is the origin of preschool children's beliefs in the reversibility of complex processes and the permeability of solid objects: are the children revealing a latent (and suppressed) credulity toward unusual properties of space and time, or is this credulity simply induced and inspired by the experimenter who is acting in a credulous fashion? This problem touches on the general question of 'revelation vs. inspiration' of various capacities in the child in the course of experimentation. The question is of a very speculative nature because there are no adequate methods for revealing the child's 'latent' capacities which do not run the risk of inspiring those same capacities at the very moment of testing. However, it is much more reasonable to view the recurrence of capacities and beliefs that dominated the child's mind at an earlier point in time, as their 'reactivation' rather than their 'inspiration'. This is especially true of the child's beliefs in nonphysical properties of object, causality, space and time, as they can be detected even in very young infants (Piaget, 1937a).

Two more reasons (one theoretical, and the other empirical) testify in favour of the 'revelation' or 'reactivation' hypothesis and against the 'inspiration' hypothesis. First, it is theoretically impossible to accept that only one of two opposite structures (for example, physical causality or belief in irreversibility of time) can be present in the child's mind without its being complemented in some way by its counterpart (magical causality, belief in reversibility of time). Second, the very facility with which children accepted the experimenter's suggestion that the box and the water was 'magical' reveal a kind of 'readiness' in the child's mind to accept such an interpretation (compare, for example, the time and effort needed in order to teach children genuinely 'inspired' concepts, such as addition–subtraction principles). However, it is widely assumed that the preschool child adopts a 'rational' stance with respect to fundamental properties of space and time such as the impermeability of solid bodies and the irreversibility of complex processes. In this study, we attempted to call this widespread assumption into question.

Chapter 5

Individual consciousness as a system of realities

The structure of individual consciousness is not one of the most popular topics in developmental psychology. This may be accounted for by the vagueness of the subject, since consciousness seems to be everything and nothing at the same time. The infinite variety of individual subjectivity has brought about numerous classifications in psychology, which deal with some of its manifestations: sensation, perception, thinking, imagination, emotion, volition, personality are distinguished. Dreams, hallucinations and children's games are regarded as manifestations of consciousness as well. Each of these manifestations is so complicated and interesting in itself that it can engage all the researcher's attention. That is why the development of psychology has always followed the path of diverging trends, and the study of separate areas.

Nevertheless, the founders of experimental psychology realized full well that a distinction of this kind was no more than a mere abstraction. In spite of the necessary and unavoidable 'dismantling' of consciousness, it was clear enough that in the absolute majority of its manifestations, from a realized sensation to a creative discovery and moral act, a human being is expressed as an integrity, as a feeling, imagining, willing, experiencing, etc., individual – in other words, a creature endowed with consciousness. Hence the question naturally arises: How to describe, 'comprehend' in concepts, understand and study this integrity? Is it possible at all to describe and study experimentally consciousness and not thinking, emotions, personality or its other manifestations? The search for the subject of the study through determining the 'general' for all the variety of the manifestations of consciousness, through a mechanic subtraction of the 'divergent properties' results in the situation where the subject of consciousness simply vanishes. Does this account for the fact that the influential psychological concepts of the twentieth century, claiming to describe a human being as an integrity based themselves not upon consciousness, but upon its individual manifestations (habits and reflexes in the theory of learning, needs and motives in psychoanalysis, thinking in cognitive psychology) and described all the rest as complicated variations of the reflexes, libido or cognitive schemes?

Nevertheless, research into ethnopsychology suggests other conclusions. Seminal studies by Edward Taylor, James Frazer, Emile Durkheim, Lucien Lévy-Brühl and E. Evans-Pritchard demonstrated the presence of various orientations in the mind of an individual. These studies resulted in distinguishing the structures in the psyche that are, in fact, absolutely independent 'elements' of consciousness and, at the same time, determine the specific features of its other elements (perception, thinking, memory, emotions, etc.); moreover, the characteristic feature of these structures unites all the elements of consciousness, as if orienting them in 'one direction' and integrating them into a single whole. These structures (here we term them fundamental structures of consciousness) are human notions of the object, causality, space and time.

The term 'notion' is, no doubt, arbitrary in this context as it is not a question of 'mental notion' or 'verbal definition', but of the structures that determine the contents of that which is realized (and experienced), while existing as subconscious. The Kantian term 'a priori forms' is far more suitable as far as the fundamental structures of consciousness are concerned. These a priori forms, while immanent to this or that cultural orientation, are reproduced in the consciousness of the individual and determine its structure. Consciousness can perform its specific 'work' – to separate the true from the false, the existing from the seeming, being from non-being – only on the basis of these forms.

Furthermore, cardinally different fundamental structures of consciousness and, consequently, principally different systems (of the orientation) of consciousness, are possible (and do exist). More than that, since these differences in the fundamental structures of consciousness are mutually complementary they should coexist in one and the same individual consciousness. Not only will 'primitive' individuals, in so far as they think and act independently of collective representations, act and argue fairly reasonably and logically, but the opposite is true as well: beliefs in magic and witchcraft have been widespread among Europeans until

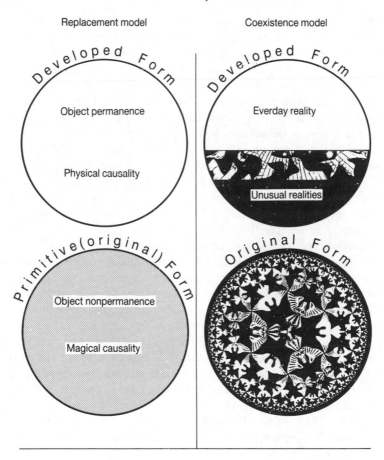

Figure 5.1 Linear and nonlinear perspectives in understanding of the development of mind © 1960 M. C. Escher/Cordon Art-Baarn-Holland

recently, and they still exist even among educated classes in the post-industrial countries: 'In reality . . . our mental activities are simultaneously rational and irrational. The prelogical and mystical elements coexist in it with the logical' (Levy-Brühl, 1925).

Due to the studies of anthropologists, the idea of the pluralistic structure of the human mind gained recognition among psychologists (Freud, 1966; Werner, 1948; Cole and Scribner, 1974; Tul'viste, 1991; Wertsch,

1991). The belief in a 'replacement model' in mental development, which dominated the psychology of the nineteenth century, was eventually replaced by a more complex 'coexistence model', which acknowledges the coexistence of recent and archaic layers in the human mind (Figure 5.1).

As a result, the individual consciousness (or reality) has been revealed as an independent entity that has its self-sufficient subject of research (the forms of existence of fundamental structures in the mind), its own specific function (the attribution of existence), and its own structure, which is not reflected in traditional classifications (the spheres of consciousness, resting on the principally different fundamental structures of consciousness).

However, this approach has so far been limited by the study of 'collective notions' and collective (social) consciousness, with a few exceptions. Developmental psychology has been influenced by the 'coexistence model' to a lesser extent. Consequently, a thorough study of the development of the 'microcosm' – the individual consciousness – within the developed collective consciousness is on the agenda. What is the consciousness of a newborn child, a baby, a toddler, a preschool and school-age child, an adult? What are their structural differences? In what way do these differences determine the process of attribution of existence to the objects and phenomena of the outer world?

In other words, it is a question of description and experimental analysis of fundamental structures of consciousness in children of various ages (and in adults too, within limits). So far we know of a single attempt of this kind, undertaken by Jean Piaget in his *La Construction du réel chez l'enfant*. This attempt – no doubt a fundamental one – was, however, limited by both the material (analysis of the development of consciousness in a child from 0 to 2 years old), and the scientific convictions of the author, consistently oriented towards the rationalistic tradition in psychology. Other studies of the child's notions of object permanence, of causality, space and time, which are numerous in the psychology of development, have been basically conducted in the traditional manner of 'divergent analysis' and resist integration into a whole. Besides, most are devoted not to the analysis of the fundamental structures of consciousness, i.e. the description and study of the oppositional notions of causality, space and time, but to the study of their particular derivatives (e.g. the child's notions of projective relations, velocity, movement, etc.).

Accordingly, several tasks have been undertaken for this study. First, it was necessary to determine the theoretical scheme for the analysis of the individual consciousness, revealing its basic structures and their cor-relations (Chapter 1). It was assumed that consciousness at all levels of ontogenesis (and not only in infancy) was, in fact, a heterogeneous, pluralistic totality combining everyday and unusual realities. Due to cultural and normative regulations, these spheres are differentiated ac-cording to the statuses of being as the child grows, with the supreme status (the completeness of being) being gradually ascribed to the every-day reality.

At the same time, the borders between the spheres of realities are not absolute: emerging initially at the level of verbal behaviour, they are not fixed at the level of real actions, remaining rather obscure at the pre-school age. It was assumed, therefore, that under certain circumstances, children can admit the norms inherent in unusual reality into the sphere of everyday reality and assimilate the phenomena relying on the fundamental structures typical of the fairy tale and play. This per-meability of the boundaries should exist in adults as well. Penetrating through this boundary, the fundamental structures of unusual reality may start to regulate the subject's real behaviour. The question, hence, consists in the study of the conditions making such a penetration possible.

The second task of this experimental study was to specify the existen-tial status of the phenomenon or the 'appearance' at the level of real behaviour with respect to the fundamental structures. The task was based on the hypothesis that even if children verbally recognized the falsity of a certain phenomenon, under certain conditions they were nevertheless apt to act in accordance with the appearance, rather than with the verbally acknowledged 'truth'.

The first step in the verification of these hypotheses was the study of the development of a permanent object in ontogenesis (Chapter 2). The particular significance of this problem stems from the fact that a perma-nent object is the most fundamental structure of individual conscious-ness, whereas elementary notions of time, space, logic, causality, reflect various aspects of the interrelationships between the objects.

In contrast to Piaget's view on object permanence development as a substitution of the impermanence norm by the permanence norm, it was assumed that both the impermanence and the permanence norms were categorical oppositions and coexisted in children's consciousness (and in adults' as well), although their 'spheres of influence' were different. The permanence norm dominates in the sphere of everyday reality, and the impermanence norm in the sphere of unusual reality. Under certain circumstances the impermanence norm can enter the sphere of everyday reality. In such a case, the subjects have to acknowledge they had come across a supernatural phenomenon.

To test this hypothesis I suggested that the children (4–7 years old) should watch the impermanence phenomena (a sudden disappearance, the transformation or the emergence of a stable object 'out of nothing'). With this aim in view a wooden box was used, which enabled me to carry through all three possible variations of the upset permanence of existence.

In the main session of the experiments the children were told that the box was 'taken out of the fairy tale' and is endowed with magical qualities: it could transform some objects into different ones. The experimenter suggested that the children should try to turn a piece of paper into a postage stamp, promising the latter as a reward. The experimenter left the room and secretly observed the children's behaviour.

The preliminary questions demonstrated that almost all the subjects freely admitted the possibility of spontaneous transformation, emergence and disappearance of the object in the sphere of the fairy tale, but still rejected its existence in real life. They did not believe that the box could 'magically' transform or destruct or generate material objects. However, coming across a real impermanence phenomenon most children behaved as if the disappearance, transformation or emergence of the object 'out of nothing' really occurred. If the promised postage stamp disappeared and the children were left without any reward they did not normally try to search for the postage stamp and were not in the least surprised. Instead, they would repeat the 'magical' actions of closing and opening the lid over and over again in the hope that 'the box wants to give the object back'.

This signifies that under certain circumstances the impermanence norm continues to regulate the children's real behaviour even with respect to sensorimotor objects (a postage stamp, a piece of paper). Among these conditions the most important one is the instruction of the adult, who admits that 'maybe the box is magical'. In the control group, where there were no instructions, the overwhelming majority of the children were surprised by the phenomenon of impermanence and quite actively searched for the object which had either disappeared or changed; i.e. they assimilated the phenomenon on the basis of the permanence norm.

Furthermore, it turned out that under the influence of the impermanence phenomena the children's verbal behaviour had undergone drastic changes. If prior to the watching of the phenomena all the children denied that these phenomena were possible within everyday reality, after having been confronted with impermanence, most children changed their opinion and explained the phenomenon relying on the impermanence norm. It is noteworthy that the children would more willingly admit the impermanence norm in the interpretation of the phenomenon of the spontaneous transformation than in the interpretation of the phenomena of disappearance or emergence of a material object 'out of nothing'.

Thus the resulting data confirmed the hypothesis, according to which the impermanence norm of existence applied to sensorimotor objects does not vanish from children's consciousness, but is simply expelled to the other spheres of consciousness (the fairytale, fantasy, dream, etc.). The idea is not novel in itself. What seems to be novel is the fact that under certain circumstances the impermanence of existence can be ascribed not only to a natural phenomenon, or a celestial body, but to an ordinary physical object in the sphere of everyday reality as well.

The further studies showed that the 'reanimation' of the impermanence norm in the sphere of everyday reality can be recorded even in adults. In these experiments the phenomenon of impermanence was demonstrated to adult subjects accompanied with the experimenter's attempts to influence the object with his 'sheer willpower'. The transformation of the object was performed in three variations: (1) reconstruction (the subjects put an old, ragged and torn postage stamp into the box and took out a new one of the same kind); (2) destruction (put a new postage stamp and took out the same kind, but torn and crumpled; (3) transformation (put one postage stamp in and took out an entirely different one of a larger size and a different design). It was assumed that if the subjects assimilated the phenomena relying on the permanence norm, they should assert that it was a different object; on the other hand, if they assumed that it was the same object, then they admit the possibility of the transformation of the object without any material influence, by 'sheer willpower', i.e. would rely on the impermanence norm.

The data showed that if at the beginning of the experiment the subjects were unwilling to acknowledge spontaneously a 'sheer willpower' influence upon the physical object, their estimates drastically changed when the experimenter assumed this possibility as one of his hypotheses about what had happened. At the end of the experiment, the subjects were asked to estimate the subjective probability for the existence of some 'natural' impermanent phenomena (such as UFOs). It was shown that the subjective probability for the existence of these unusual phenomena approximately coincided with the subjective probability of the transformation of the material object by 'sheer willpower'.

The cross-cultural (Russian and German samples) comparison showed that subjects' behaviour while observing impermanence phenomena varied only slightly across cultures, whereas subjects' estimations for the probabilities of existence of natural enigmatic phenomena did reflect certain cultural differences.

All the abovementioned attest to the fact that belief in the impermanence of a stable material object can be found not only in infants and children of the preschool age but in adults as well; however, this belief is only manifested under special circumstances. The most important of these circumstances is the instruction and actions of the experimenters in which the experimenter, although indirectly, acknowledges the possibility of object impermanence. If such an instruction were absent, adult subjects' consciousness resisted acknowledging the impermanence phenomenon. As the experiments showed, the subjects were more willing to change the temporal and spatial order of the events surrounding the impermanence phenomenon than to acknowledge that a physical object can spontaneously disappear or appear 'from nothing'. This shows once more that even the most fundamental of our physical beliefs (such as the belief in object permamence) are intimately linked with the recognition of these beliefs by other people.

Similar results were obtained in a series of studies on the development of causality. Although the development of this notion has been well investigated before, the available works do not answer the question whether preschool and school age children would use magical (animistic) causality while assimilating the phenomena at the level of their real (and not only verbal) behaviour. A series of experiments was conducted in which children aged 4, 5 and 6 years were asked to interpret verbally and assimilate some unusual phenomena, which incorporated the element of magical causality (a direct affect of subjectivity upon an inanimated object, or a spontaneous animation of an inanimate object).

In one case, the children were told a story about a magical box, which, under the influence of certain words, turned the pictures of the objects into real objects; in the other case, they were told a story about 'a magical table', capable of turning plastic figures of animals into real animals; in the third case, the story was about an unusual car which could move under the influence of magical words and the manipulation of its picture.

The results of the experiments confirmed that in the sphere of everyday reality children's consciousness involves both natural and animistic modes of assimilation of phenomena. At the verbal level the overwhelming majority of 4-year-olds unambiguously claimed that spontaneous animation of the objects and magical influence on the objects were impossible. The predominance of such answers testifies to the fact that children of this age group have already developed the embryonic natural scientific mode, but its psychological status can vary according to circumstances.

First, it predominates only at the level of verbal behaviour. The specificity of this level facilitates the legal norms to manifest themselves. On the one hand, verbal behaviour usually occurs in the situation of direct outward control (a conversation with an adult), which makes it profitable for the child to use the socially approved (in this case the natural scientific) norms for the assimilation of phenomena. On the other hand, the use of fundamental structures, inherent in unusual reality, in this situation is not motivated at all or is negatively motivated (the fear of being criticized or disapproved of by the adult). Second, the natural scientific presumption dominates here only in the sphere of everyday reality; in the sphere of the fairy tale all the children were unanimous in their admittance of the possibility for unusual events.

Yet another specific feature, typical of 4–5-year-old children, is the instability of the boundaries separating the sphere of everyday reality and the fairy tale at the level of verbal behaviour. Thus, after listening to a fairy tale, a significant number of children aged 4 and 5 years changed their opinion and admitted the possibility of bizarre events in the sphere of everyday reality as well; only the six-year-olds expressed unequivocal boundaries between the fairy tale and everyday reality.

An analysis of the children's real behaviour without an outward control gives quite a different picture. Even in the sphere of everyday reality magical causality is endowed with a quite strong existence: the behaviour of the majority of children spoke of their conviction of the possibility of the spontaneous transformation and magical influence upon the object.

Why do children prefer to apply the magical causality instead of relying on the physical one?

Clearly, it happens because the use of magical actions is positively motivated by the desire to obtain the attractive object quickly or avoid the imminent danger. The necessity to use physical causality to assimilate the phenomena is not substantiated from without by any external control. However, in my view, there is yet another, more profound reason. It consists in the fact that in children's minds, magical and physical causalities are not yet firmly hierarchized according to their existential statuses.

This dynamic coexistence of two opposite types of causality in children's practical behaviour was revealed most saliently in the experiments with perception of the phenomenal and rational causality: upon getting the rational 'quasi-scientific' interpretation of the transformation of water in the tubes, the children acknowledged it at the verbal level, but only a few of them relied on this information in their practical actions. Moreover, in most children the phenomenal causality very quickly superseded the rational, 'quasi-scientific' interpretation even at the level of verbal judgements.

Such a coexistence of the two types of causality can only take place under certain circumstances (hypothetically in the case of dynamic equilibrium between 'psychological weights' of phenomenal and rational perceptions). If this condition is not observed, the phenomenal causality is either ousted by the rational one from both the verbal and real behaviour, or vice versa, ousts the rational perception from the area of the verbal judgement. Presumably, this is precisely what happens to the preschoolers' beliefs in magical causality when they grow older and become subject to the growing pressure of culture.

The investigation of the junior schoolchildren's behaviour in one of the experimental conditions (the magic box) showed that the boundary between unusual and everyday reality strengthened with age: whereas the behaviour of pupils of the first grade did not essentially differ from that of the senior preschool children, the third graders acted as if they did not view the magical manipulations to be of any real value. This testifies to the view that physical causality occupies a dominant position in everyday reality at both the verbal and real levels of the children's behaviour.

Nevertheless, according to the data, in no case should magical causality be viewed as shifting to the sphere of 'pure fantasies'. Not only does it retain its legitimate status within the domain of unusual reality, but it can be reactivated in everyday reality as well. The experiments showed that if adult subjects are confronted with an insoluble problem, some of them do apply magical manipulations in order to find a solution.

The experimental data enables us to distinguish certain hypothetical stages in the development of the two modes of the assimilation of physical reality. The first stage (approximately 3–4 years) may be viewed as a preparatory one. At this stage children come across both, the magical (fairy tale) and the natural scientific causality (the explanations of the adults); however, these types of causality are not differentiated and opposed to each other either at the level of verbal judgements or in children's practical actions.

At the second stage (4–5 years) the opposition between physical and magical modes of explanation makes its first appearance in children's consciousness. On reflection, they could already separate the possible from the impossible. Correspondingly, children start to distinguish between everyday and unusual realities, with the magical mode at the verbal level being ousted into the sphere of the fairy tale and play, and the natural scientific one beginning to dominate in the sphere of everyday reality. But for all that, the boundary between the two types of reality is not yet fixed: so children, upon listening to a fairy tale, quite easily transfer its magical causality into the sphere of everyday reality, and seeing an unusual event, they interpret it as a magical one, etc. As for the level of real behaviour, the contrast norms of causality here are not yet hierarchized according to the statuses of being: that is why, with positive motivation, children can rely on both magical and physical causality in the sphere of everyday reality.

At the third stage (6–7 years), at the verbal level, the boundary between everyday and unusual realities becomes more stable, and everyday reality acquires the supreme existential status. Witnessing an unusual phenomenon, children try to localize it in time and space, thus isolating it as 'an exception', and in this way retain the boundary between the sphere of the 'magical' and the sphere of everyday reality. While explaining the impossibility of unusual phenomena children use generalizations that approach scientific ones. But, at the level of real behaviour, the strong hierarchization between spheres of realities is still absent.

Finally, at the fourth stage (about nine years of age), children assimilate unusual phenomena at both levels exclusively on the basis of the natural scientific causality, either with or without any external control. The magical causality is totally removed to the sphere of unusual reality, and the factors that brought about the reanimation of magical causality with younger children are no longer effective. At the same time, the boundary between everyday and the unusual realities is in no case absolute and, under certain circumstances, can be violated even in the consciousness of an adult.

Although this hypothesis in certain features coincides with that proposed by Piaget (for instance, in the progressive tendency for children to apply more to physical causality with age), it deviates from Piaget's picture in several important aspects.

First of all, the development of physical causality (as well as of object permanence or physical space and time) in children older than two is not viewed here as solely the *development of verbal judgements*. It is viewed as the development of fundamental structures that can *coexist* both on the verbal and real levels of behaviour, can be *transferred* from one to the other, or can *struggle* for dominance at one and the same level, but which at the same time are invariant with respect to levels of behaviour and exist in their own right.

A similar 'competitive coexistence' may occur (and according to certain data, does occur) even within the first two years of the children's life. However, since the verbal level of behaviour does not exist in a young infant and is not yet fully developed in a young child, the dynamic competition between various types of causality can be only observed here through the children's real (sensorimotor) behaviour. In fact, Piaget's description of the development of consciousness within the first two years of life is also a description of the coexistence of the opposite types of fundamental structures. Piaget shifts, however, from the 'coexistence model' to the 'replacement model' whenever he approaches the starting and the end points of this period, whereas according to the recent data, the opposite fundamental structures of mind should be viewed as coexisting with one another *from the very beginning*.

Thus, the two opposite types of causality are presented not as their consistent substitution of one another (which is neither theoretically nor practically possible), but as a simultaneous movement in a specific 'two-sided psychological space' of consciousness, one side of which is the differentiation between spheres of realities and the other its functioning at different levels (the involved level and the uninvolved level). In the total account, magical causality emerging simultaneously with natural causality and initially coexisting with the latter is gradually ousted into the sphere of unusual reality; as for the physical one, it dominates in the sphere of everyday reality. Initially, this hierarchization occurs at the level of verbal behaviour and then at the level of real behaviour. None the less, it should be taken into account that differentiation of the various types of causality according to spheres should not be understood literally: being one of the fundamental structures, magical and physical causalities, while being divided in the child's consciousness according to the statuses of being, are at the same time creating these spheres of realities themselves.

Simultaneously with the differentiation between the spheres of consciousness and the hierarchization of their existential statuses, the stratification and the differentiation inside the sphere of everyday reality occurs. With the appearance of rational constructions, children develop a new form of the presentation of the outer world, and with it the problem of existentialization arises. The research of this problem shows that as children grow, they begin to differentiate between appearance and reality quite easily and identify the rational constructions of the object with 'reality' and the phenomena with 'appearance'.

However, some of the studies presented here have demonstrated that reducing the phenomenon to 'appearance' as a universal process in the development of existentialization occurs only at the level of verbal behaviour. At the level of the real actions, this process is more sophisticated and complex. Sometimes the phenomenon, while being recognized verbally as an 'appearance' (i.e., as an illusion devoid of completeness of being), actually stops regulating the behaviour of children at the level of real actions (this is true, among other things, of the phenomenon of the perception of the long row as containing more elements as compared to the short one). In other cases it continues regulating the actions of children in spite of verbal devaluation (for example, the perception of one of two identical rulers as the longer one against the background of the Mueller–Layer arrow illusion (see Subbotsky, 1990).

The most plausible description of the interrelationships between opposite fundamental structures, which, unlike ordinary knowledge, can never disappear from consciousness, is that of 'coexistence'. The archaic structures, being exiled in the scope of unusual realities, are waiting for the appropriate circumstances to reappear in everyday reality again. This concerns not only object permanence and causality, but the fundamental properties of space and time as well.

Although, according to some data, the differentiation between permeable and impermeable as well as an ability to detect irreversibility of events are manifest even in babies in their first months of life, these structures exist only in practical actions of infants and cannot be viewed as concepts. By the age of three the child develops a stable understanding of the fundamental structures of space and time that is, however, still mainly nonverbal. The picture drastically changes by the age of four, at which, according to my data, the impossibility of violating the impermeability of solid bodies or the irreversibility of the complex processes through the volition effort or magic words are generally accepted. It means that the unusual qualities of space and time are applied by the children solely to the sphere of unusual reality whereas impermeability and irreversibility seem to them to be inseparable features of real life.

None the less, it turned out that under the influence of an adult's instruction some children acted as though the permeability of solid objects for other solid objects depends upon their own will. The similar influence substantiated by watching the unusual phenomenon resulted in the animation of the children's belief in the reversibility of complex processes.

Thus properties of space and time, typical of these structures in the sphere of the fairy tale, permeate the sphere of everyday reality and begin to regulate children's real behaviour. At the same time, it was found that the rigidity of the boundaries separating unusual properties of space and time from everyday reality intensified with age, which corresponded to the data yielded in previous studies with respect to the object and causality concepts.

On the whole, the data testify to the view that the development of individual consciousness does not correspond to the 'replacement model', rather it matches the opposite 'coexistence model', which assumes differentiation between the spheres of realities and their hierarchization according to the statuses of being. This differentiation occurs at different rates at various levels of behaviour and is determined by various factors. The establishing of these factors in the studies presented in this book, although very incomplete and insufficient, might, nevertheless, be viewed as a step towards the experimental research of the development of individual consciousness. Although, basically, the studies were theoretically oriented, however, certain *implications for scientific education* might also be drawn out.

First, the results of the study may put under question the legitimacy of the overwhelming tendency of a contemporary school education to put emphasis on scientific subjects at the expense of the subjects related to the unusual spheres of consciousness (fine arts, science fiction, studies of fantasies and dreams, imaginative role play, etc.). Since children in their mature years are not going to live exclusively within the sphere of everyday reality but in the sphere of unusual reality as well, it might be desirable to prepare them for this by giving more room in the school curriculum to subjects like psychology, theory of dreams, theory of art, mythology, science fiction, etc.

Moreover, since certain functions of unusual realities (e.g., materialization of unrealized wishes, resurrecting function) are expected to have positive influence on the development of healthy personality and even (the constructive function) on the development of rational thinking in the child, it seems highly desirable to cultivate in schoolchildren the development of fantasy to a degree comparable with that of the development of logical and thinking skills.

Another possible implication concerns the interrelationships between verbal and real levels of behaviour in education. On the one hand, since contemporary school education is basically 'verbal', attention must be paid to the means that could provide new knowledge with the necessary 'psychological weight' so that it would not be ousted from children's minds by the more 'phenomenologically persuasive' representations acquired by the children prior to the 'educational impact'. The danger for scientific education of becoming merely 'verbal' and 'formal' has been highlighted in many studies (in particular, those by Piaget and Vygotsky); however, even verbal knowledge, if properly given, can influence children's real behaviour. What the means are of making the new knowledge salient enough (and the old one weak enough) to secure this influence is, of course, the problem to be studied in each particular case.

On the other hand, the complete lack of interest in the fate of 'out of date' and rejected representations which can be observed in a prevailing rationalistic approach to scientific education doesn't seem to be psychologically adequate either. Since beliefs in magic and object nonpermanence cannot (and should not) be ultimately eradicated from children's minds, they must be given a certain 'place' and even cultivated, rather than just declared 'false' and forgotten. This 'place' can be easily found in myths, dreams and science fiction. Even more particular 'false' representations, such as those that are being replaced by the laws of mechanics or thermodynamics, must not be forgotten. They might be 'placed' in special 'alternative textbooks' in which objects and things do not obey ordinary physical laws. This permanent 'comparison by contrast' could not only make school scientific education more interesting and animated, it would also correspond better to the intimate laws of the child's consciousness.

It seems that it is just the neglect of these intimate laws that leads to the ease with which many adult educated persons can under certain circumstances discount even the most fundamental physical beliefs (such as belief in object permanence). The popularity of superstitions, beliefs in various supernatural and anomalous phenomena, etc. in contemporary industrial cultures can be explained by, among other factors, the ineffectiveness of rationalistically oriented scientific education, the final result of which is much more fragile than it is usually supposed to be. Deprived of the developed areas for legal existence, the unusual fundamental structures find their place within the domain of everyday reality, thus undermining its very foundation.

In more general terms it might be assumed that viewing the development of individual consciousness through the prism of 'replacement' and 'coexistence' perspectives to a certain extent reflects the paths of European psychology.

The distinction between spheres of realities dates back to the Scepticism of Antiquity. For the Sceptics, the principal problem was the impossibility of establishing any stable criteria for the distinction between the spheres of reality – everyday reality, a night dream, a myth – although everything that occurred in these spheres evidently contradicted each other. Thus Anaxogorus and Monim 'compared the existing with the scenery in the theatre and considered the existing to be similar to that which happens in a night dream or madness' (Sextus Empiricus, 1976, p. 11).

Although this comparison is on the difference between everyday and unusual realities (e.g. vigil and night dream), none the less, neither the parameters of differentiation nor the criteria of hierarchy between these spheres (in which of them the world is given as 'true' and in which as 'false') are determined. Moreover, the impossibility of finding a logical criterion, distinguishing everyday reality from the unusual one, is clearly realized.

While situating everyday reality as opposed to mythological reality, Plato determined certain parameters for the differentiation. Thus, in his myth of the universe, there exist two interesting implications: the reversibility of the sequence (of time), and the possibility of verbal communication between people and animals (Plato, *Statesman*, 1952, pp. 270a–271e). However, the reality of the myth is not regarded by Plato as 'subordinated' (untrue) in relation to everyday reality. Moreover, the possibility of extraordinary events is admitted in the sphere of everyday reality, e.g. magic and prophesy (Plato, *Laws*, 1952, Book XI, p. 933d, e), the movement of the planets are subject to reason (ibid., pp. 781–2).

The criteria responsible for the specific features of everyday reality were most consistently worked out by Aristotle in his *Metaphysics* and particularly in his *Logic*. Aristotle determined everyday reality as a set of stable, discrete objects, assigned permanence and mutually connected through causal ties (at the level of logic – through the necessity of sequence). Imagination and night dreams differ from everyday reality according to these parameters, as in imagination and dreams the distinctions between the false and the true vanish and the objects obey our thought. In their turn, imagination and night dreams are also distinguished according to the criterion of 'involvement'. In a night dream 'when something seems to terrify or frighten us, we instantly experience terror or fear, or accordingly when something calms us down. And when we are imagining our state is similar to that when we are examining a picture featuring something terrible and soothing' (Aristotle, 1952, p. 660).

Lastly Aristotle points to a clear hierarchy between the spheres of reality, postulating the primacy for everyday reality. He subjects myths to a logical analysis and demonstrates their inherent contradictions. In his opinion, 'those who present their wisdom in the form of myths are not worthy of serious attention' (Aristotle, 1952, p. 519). The same is true for night dreams. Although dreams and everyday reality cannot be differentiated logically, the very fact that we seek the differentiating criteria in the state of vigilance determines the advantage and primacy of everyday reality.

None the less, the boundary between everyday reality and unusual reality remained vague until the epoch of modern history. Nickolas of Cusan (fifteenth century), although discussing the fundamentals of science, still admitted magic and the kinship of human beings with spirits. Francis Bacon included in the fundamentals of sciences the axioms of mathematics, logic and physics, and postulated the permanence of the physical object in particular ('everything changes, but nothing disappears'). He rejected natural magic as unscientific, equating it with dreams, hallucinations and fantasy; magic, astrology and alchemy are based on 'imagination and faith' and break the basic units of everyday reality: the impossibility of the direct realization of subjectivity and the irreversibility of time. Nevertheless in the fundamentals of his 'primary philosophy' he also includes the so-called 'natural theology' – the theory of angels and spirits (Bacon, *Primary Philosophy*, 1968, p. 536).

Only with the emergence of consistent rationalism, was the sphere of everyday reality constituted by way of prohibition on the direct accessibility of an alien subjectivity. For Locke (1632–1704), 'the angels of all kinds . . . are beyond the bound of our cognition' (Locke, 1961, Vol. II p. 162). Descartes (1596–1650) distinguished the permanence of objects as a major parameter, separating everyday reality from dreams: 'if somebody appears suddenly before me when I am vigilant and disappears just as unexpectedly, and I could not note where he came from and left for as it usually happens to images I see in my dreams, I would consider him, not without grounds, a ghost or an apparition, created by my brain and similar to those appearing in it when I sleep, rather than a living man' (Descartes, 1950, p. 103). Closely following the basic argument of the Sceptics, Descartes solves the problem by pointing out the very fact of the presence of logic in the sphere of everyday reality and the weakness of it in a dream: everyday reality is 'true', but the dream is 'false' as 'our reasoning in our sleep can never be so evident or complete as in vigil, although imagination can sometimes be more lively and expressive' (*ibid.*, p. 54).

Developing the line of Descartes and Locke, Kant analysed in greater detail the conditions and limitations in the sphere of everyday reality (or 'nature'), calling them 'a priori fundamentals' of reason. Among others, these include: the permanence of objects ('only changes exist, but not an emergence out of nothing'), continuity of their links (there cannot be any vacuum between two phenomena), a universal conditionality of nature by physical causes (nothing happens arbitrarily). The means of organization of everyday reality is science, while everything that constitutes the 'internal' of things is placed outside the cognizable, in the sphere of faith.

Dream, myth, religion are not included in the sphere of scientific knowledge. For Kant everyday reality is the superior type of reality. Only that which is accessible to experience and contemplation can fully exist, while all the rest, including the regulative ideas of reason (ideas of the world, God, Ego, the 'thing in its own right'), is important only to the extent it is useful for the organization and ordering of the objects of experience (Kant, 1965). Later on, the hierarchization of the realities, grounded by Kant, is constantly preserved. Thus, Hegel regards Absolute Spirit as a subject of science: dreams, fantasy, ecstasy should be rejected for the sake of reason (Hegel, 1913). It is also important to note that the unusual realities of consciousness *per se* have never been analysed within the framework of classical thought. The tendency was persistent, and in the nineteenth century the focus of European philosophy (and the psychology that grew from the latter) was increasingly reduced to an investigation of everyday reality. It was not until the twentieth century that the traditional neglect of the spheres of unusual reality began to fade. The impetus for the change came from various sources.

It was becoming ever more evident that both the real life of society (economic, political and social) and the individual psychology of a human being cannot be kept within the bounds of the rational constructions elaborated in advance (the ideas, schemes or long-term projects, etc.). Even more obvious was the fact that the life of the consciousness could not be reduced to the constructions of reason, embracing not only the world of nature, but society and the world of the consciousness *per se* as well. It became clear that a part (and quite a significant part at that) of a human being dwells not in the world of everyday reality, but in the world of dreams, fantasy, play, etc.

In both science and art a point was made of the role of intuitive processes in the subconscious, and the mythology of the twentieth century engendered totalitarian regimes and wars, compared to which Sparta was just a trifle and the Trojan episode was nothing but a voyage. The demand for illusion brought about a variety of creations such as scientific fiction, cinema, television, computer games and drug addiction.

Freud was one of the first to draw the attention of psychologists to the significance of fantasy, night dreams and myths. It was not the addressing of the unusual spheres of consciousness *per se* that was of primary importance – in fact, it had happened even before that – but giving to them the existential status comparable with that of everyday reality. The achievements of psychoanalysis were developed both in psychology and other spheres as well (philosophy, literature and the art of avant-garde).

However, the recognition of the fact that a human being can live in a world where the laws of everyday reality are violated cannot but attract the attention of scientists of the humanitarian spheres to those fundamental structures that underlie unusual realities of consciousness. Due to a strange (but probably not accidental) coincidence, at the same time fundamental structures of consciousness have become the object for a thorough study by the natural sciences, particularly by physics (Mamardashvili, Soloviev and Shvyrev, 1970; Prigogine and Stengers, 1986).

The formulation of the theory of elementary particles, the discovery of the uncertainty principle, altered the traditional view of causality and physical object, and the theory of relativity shattered the notions of space and time. The transition from investigating macro-objects, in the course of the description of which the contribution of subjectivity is so minimal that it could possibly be ignored, to the investigation of micro-objects resulted in the role of the a priori forms of consciousness growing immensely. The object of the study was no longer a phenomenon given directly, but a system of rational constructions, built on the basis of indirectly given phenomena. Moreover, the thoroughly elaborated methods for this indirect 'completion' of the visible universe clashed with the fundamental limitations: it became impossible, for instance, to set simultaneously the impulse and the trajectory of the electron's motion due to the unavoidable loss of information in the course of its transformation into the forms, accessible for perception.

The notion of causality underwent drastic changes. Whereas classical physics acknowledges the existence of probabilistic laws in the phenomenal world, but not in the world of rational constructions, non-classical physics had to introduce the element of uncertainty in the description of the object itself, i.e. to admit that physical causality as a rational construction is not able to give an exhaustive account of the interactions in the worlds of the elementary particles. All this cannot but direct researchers' attention away from phenomena and rational constructions towards consciousness, to those fundamental structures which underlie intuitions on the object as such: causality, time and space. It is even more evident now that without a detailed clarification of these structures any further advance 'inside the matter' will be halted by fundamental obscurities and paradoxes.

The principal purpose of this clarification consists in understanding in what way and for what reasons from all the variety of mental events a human being selects something and makes this very 'something' a reference-point for his or her judgement and behaviour. In other words, the purpose is, in fact, the description of the methods and means for the attribution of existence. As these methods are specific for human beings of different ages one of the aspects of the problem of existentialization, and what is more, the purely psychological aspect, is the description of the fundamental structures of the child's consciousness and their development throughout the life-span.

Bibliography

Aristotle (1952) *The Works*. In *Great Books of the Western World*, Chicago–Toronto–Geneva: Encyclopaedia Britannica.

Aristotle (1976) *Works*, in four volumes, Vol. 1, Moscow: Mysl Publ.

Aristotle (1978) *Works*, in four volumes, Vol. 2, Moscow: Mysl Publ.

Arnheim, R. (1954) *Art and Visual Perception. A Psychology of the Creative Eye*, Berkeley–Los Angeles: University of California Press.

Arseniev, A. S. (1980). *Myshlenije psichologa i problema litchnosty* (Psychologist's thinking and the problem of personality). Moscow, unpublished manuscript.

Bacon, F. (1968) *The Works of Francis Bacon*, collected and edited by James Spelding, Robert Leslie Ellis and Doughlas Denon Heath, Vol. IV, New York: Garret Press.

Baillargeon, R. (1987) 'Object permanence in 3½- and 4½-month-old infants', *Developmental Psychology, 23*, pp. 655–64.

Baillargeon, R., Spelke, E. S. and Wassermann, S. (1985) 'Object permanence in five-month-old infants', *Cognition, 20*, pp. 191–208.

Beveridge, M. and Davies, M. (1983) 'A picture-sorting approach to the study of child animism'. In *Genetic Psychology Monographs*, 107, pp. 211–31.

Bower, T. G. R. (1971) 'The object in the world of the infant'. In *Scientific American, 225*(4), pp. 30–8.

Bower, T. G. R. (1974) *Development in Infancy*, San Francisco: Freeman.

Brain, M. D. S. and Shanks, B. L. (1965) 'The conservation of shape property and proposal about the origin of conservation'. In *Canadian Journal of Psychology, 19*, pp. 197–207.

Bremner, J. G. (1991) *Infancy*, Oxford and Cambridge, Mass.: Basil Blackwell.

Bühler, K. (1930) *Die geistige Entwicklung des Kindes*, Jena: Gustav Fischer.

Bullock, M. (1984) 'Preschool children's understanding of causal connections'. In *British Journal of Developmental Psychology, 2*, pp. 139–48.

Bullock, M. (1985) 'Animism in childhood thinking: a new look at an old question'. In *Developmental Psychology, 21*(2), pp. 217–25.

Bullock, M. and Gelman, R. (1979) 'Preschool children's assumptions about cause and effect: temporal ordering', *Child Development, 50, 1*, pp. 89–96.

Butterworth, G. (1975) 'Object identity in infancy: the interaction of spatial location codes in determining search errors', *Child Development, 46*(4), pp. 866–70.

Carey, S. (1985) *Conceptual Change in Childhood*, Cambridge, Mass.: Bradford Books, MIT Press.

Cole, M. and Scribner, S. (1974) *Culture and Thought. A Psychological Introduction*, New York–London–Sydney–Toronto: John Wiley & Sons.

Cossette-Ricard, M. (1983) 'L'Identité de l'object chez le jeune enfant'. In *Archives de Psychologie*, monogr. 9, Geneva, pp. 261–325.

Descartes, R. (1950) *Jsbrannije proisvedevija* (Collected Works), Moscow: Gospolitizdat.

Descartes, R. (1952) *Great Books of the Western World*, 31: *Descartes, Spinoza*, Chicago–Toronto–Geneva: Encyclopaedia Britannica.

El'konin, D. B. (1978) *Psikhologija igzy* (Psychology of Play), Moscow: Pedagogica Publ.

Evans-Pritchard, E. E. (1937) *Witchcraft, Oracles and Magic among the Azande*, Oxford: Clarendon Press.

Flavell, J. H. (1986) 'The develoment of children's knowledge about the appearance–reality distinction. In *American Psychologist*, April, *41*(4), pp. 418–25.

Flavell, J. H., Flavell, E. R. and Green, F. L. (1985a) *Young Children's Knowledge about the Appearant – Real and Pretend – Real Distinctions*, unpubl. manuscript, Stanford University, California.

Flavell, J. H., Green, F. L., Wahl, K. E. and Flavell, E. R. (1985b) *The Effects of Question Clarification and Memory Aids on Young Children's Performance on Appearance–Reality Tasks*, unpubl. manuscript, Stanford University, California.

Freeman, N. H., Lloyd, S. and Sinha, C. G. (1980) 'Infant search tasks reveal early concepts of containment and canonical usage of objects', *Cognition, 8*(3), pp. 243–62.

Freud, S. (1924) *Psikhologija sna* (Psychology of dreaming), Moscow: Sovremennije Problemy Publ.

Freud, S. (1966) *Introductory Lectures on Psychoanalysis*, New York: Liveright Publishers Co.

Gibson, J. J. *The Ecological Approach to Visual Perception*, Boston: Houghton Mifflin.

Gibson, E. J., Owsley, C. J., Walker, A. and Megaw-Nyce, J. (1979) 'Development of the perception of invariants: substance and shape', In *Perception, 8*, pp. 609–19.

Gibson, E. J. and Walk, R. D. (1960) 'The visual cliff', *Scientific American, 202*, 64–71.

Gibson, E. J. and Walker, A. S. (1984) 'Development of knowledge of visual-tactual affordances of substance'. In *Child Development, 55*, pp. 453–60.

Girnis, S. V. (1985) *Vosprijatije detmi mladshego shkolnogo vozrasta neobychnych phisicheskich javlienij* (Perception of the unusual physical phenomena by junior school children), a diploma project, Moscow University, Department of Psychology, unpubl. manuscript.

Golinkoff, R. M., Barding, C. G., Carlson, V. and Sexton, M. E. (1984) 'The infant's perception of causal events: the distinction between animate and inanimate objects'. In *Advances in Infancy Research*, Vol. 3, Lipsitt, L. P. and Rovee-Collier, C. (eds), Norwood, N.Y.: Ablex Publishing Corporation, pp. 145–65.

Goods, N. S. (1982) 'Is before really easier to understand than after?' In *Child Development, 53*(3), pp. 822–5.

Gottfried, A. W. and Rose, S. A. (1980) 'Tactile recognition memory in infants'. In *Child Development, 51*(1), pp. 69–74.

Gouin Décarie, T. (1974) *Intelligence and Affectivity in Early Childhood. An experimental study of Jean Piaget's object concept and object relations*, New York: International University Press.

Gratch, G. (1982) 'Responses to hidden persons and things by 5-, 9-, and 16-month-old infants in a visual tracking situation'. In *Developmental Psychology, 18*(2), pp. 232–7.

Gratch, G. and Landers, W. F. (1971) 'Stage IV Piaget's theory of infants' object concepts: a longitudinal study', *Child Development, 42*(2), pp. 359–72.

Gregory, R. L. (1980) *The Intelligent Eye*, London: Weidenfeld & Nicolson.

Grivtsov, A. P. (1988) *Vlijanie emotcionalnogo sostojanija na povedenije cheloveka v situatcii nerazreshimoj zadachi* (The influence of the emotional state on human behaviour in a situation of unsoluble problem), unpublished research project, Moscow University, Department of Psychology.

Hagleitner, L. (1983) 'Der sogenannte Animismus beim Kind'. In *Praxis und Kinderpsychologie, 32*, pp. 261–6.

Haith, M. M. and Campos, J. J. (1977) 'Human infancy', *Annual Review of Psychology, 28*, pp. 251–93.

Hamer, R. D., Alexander, K. R. and Teller, D. J. 'Rayleigh Discriminations in Young Human Infants'. In *Vision Research, 22*(5), pp. 575–87.

Harris, P. L. (1973) 'Perseverative errors in search by young infants', *Child Development, 44*(1), pp. 28–33.

Harris, P. L. (1975) 'Development of search and object permanence during infancy', *Psychological Bulletin, 82*(3), pp. 332–44.

Harris, P. (1985) 'The development of search'. In P. Salapatek and L. B. Cohen (eds), *Handbook of Infant Perception*, New York: Academic Press.

Harris, P. L. (1991) 'Commentary', *Human Development, 34*, pp. 138–42.

Harris, P. L., Brown, E., Marriott, C., Whittall, S. and Harmer, S. (1991) 'Monsters, ghosts and witches: Testing the limits of the fantasy–reality distinction in young children', *British Journal of Developmental Psychology*, 9, pp. 105–23.

Hegel, G. (1973) *Phenomenologija Ducha* (Phenomenology of the Spirit). In *Works of the Philosophical Society of Saint Petersburg*, 8.

Hochberg, J. (1971) 'Perception. Space and movement'. In Woodworth and Schlosberg (eds), *Experimental Psychology*. London: Methuen, pp. 475–550.

Huang, I. (1930) 'Children's explanations of strange phenomena'. In *Psychologische Forschung*, 14, pp. 63–183.

Inhelder, B. and Piaget, J. (1969) *The Early Growth of Logic in the Child*, New York and London: W. W. Norton.

Jersild, A. T. and Holmes, F. B. (1935) 'Methods of overcoming children's fears'. In *The Journal of Psychology*, 1, pp. 75–104.

Johnson, C and Harris, P. L. (1992) 'Magic: Special but not excluded' (submitted).

Johnson, C. N. and Wellman, H. M. (1980) 'Children's developing understanding of mental verbs: remember, know, and guess'. In *Child Development, 51*(4), pp. 1095–102.

Johnson, C. N. and Wellman, H. M. (1982) 'Children's developing conceptions of the mind and brain'. In *Child Development, 53*(1), pp. 222–34.

Kant, I. (1965) *Works*, in six volumes, Vol 3, Moscow: Mysl Publ.

Keil, F. (1979) 'The development of the young child's ability to anticipate the outcomes of simple causal events', *Child Development, 50*(2), pp. 455–62.

Kohler, J. (1970) 'The formation and transformation of the visual world'. In R. N. Haber (ed.), *Contemporary Theory and Research in Visual Perception*, London–New-York–Sydney–Toronto: Holt, Rinehart & Winston, pp. 474–97.

Krippner, S. (1986) 'Dreams and the development of a personal mythology', *Journal of Mind & Behavior, 7*(2–3), pp. 449–61.

Kun, A. (1978) 'Evidence for preschoolers' understanding of causal direction in extended causal sequence', *Child Development, 49*(1), pp. 218–22.

Laurendeau, M. and Pinard, A. (1962) *Causal Thinking in the Child*, Montreal: International University Press.

LeCompte, G. K. and Gratch, G. (1972) 'Violation of a rule as a method diagnosing infant's level of object concept', *Child Development, 43* (2), pp. 385–96.

Leontiev, A. N. (1977) *Activity. Consciousness. Personality*, Moscow: Politizdat Publ.

Leslie, A. M. (1982) 'The perception of causality in infants', *Perception, 11*(2), pp. 173–86.

Leslie, A. M. (1984) 'Infant perception of manual pick-up event', *British Journal of Development Psychology*, 2, pp. 29–32.

Leslie, A. (1986) 'Getting development off the ground. Modularity and infant's perception of causality'. In P. L. C. van Geert (ed.), *Theory Building in*

Developmental Psychology, Amsterdam: Elsevier Science Publishers B.V. (North-Holland), pp. 405–37.

Levin, I. (1979) 'Interference of time-related and unrelated cues with duration comparisons of young children: analysis of Piaget's formulation of the relation of time and speed', *Child Development, 50*(2), pp. 469–77.

Levin, I. and Gilat, I. (1983). 'A developmental analysis of early time concepts: the equivalence and additivity of the effect of interfering cues on duration comparisons of young children', *Child Development, 54*(1), pp. 78–83.

Levin, I., Israeli, E. and Darom, E. (1978) 'The development of time concepts in young children: the relations between duration and succession', *Child Development, 49*(3), pp. 755–64.

Levin, K. (1935) *A dynamic Theory of Personality*, New York and London: McGraw-Hill.

Lévy-Brühl, L. (1925) *La Mentalité primitive*, Paris: Alcan.

Locke, J. (1961) *An Essay Concerning Human Understanding*, in two volumes, London: L. Dent, M. Y. Datton.

Lucas, T. C. and Uzgiris, I. C. (1977) 'Spatial factors in the development of the object concept', *Developmental Psychology, 13*(5), pp. 492–500.

Luger, G. F., Bower, T. G. R. and Wishart, J. G. (1983) 'A model of the development of the early infant object concept', *Perception, 12*(1), pp. 21–34.

Luger, G. F., Wishart, J. G. and Bower, T. G. R. (1984) 'Modelling the stages of the identity theory of object-concept development in infancy'. *Perception, 13*, pp. 97–115.

Mamardashvili, M. K. (1984) *Klassicheskij i neklassicheski idealy razionalnosty* (Classical and nonclassical ideals of rationality), Tbilisi: Metsniereba Publ.

Mamardashvili, M. K., Soloviev, E. U. and Shvyrev, V. S. (1970) *Klassicheskaya i sovrernennaja buzguaznaja philosophija* (Classical and modern bourgeois philosophy) Voprosy philosophii, *12*, pp. 23–38.

Mead, M. (1932) 'An investigation of the thought of primitive children, with special reference to animism', *Journal of the Royal Anthropological Institute, 62*, pp. 173–90.

Meider, M. and Gratch, G. (1980) Do 5-month-olds show object conception in Piaget's sense?' In *Infant Behavior and Development, 3*, pp. 265–82.

Meulemann, H. (1985) 'Säkularisierung und Politik. Wertwandel und Wertstruktur in der Bundesrepublik Deutschland', *Politische Vierteljahresschrift, 26*, pp. 29–51.

Michotte, A. (1962) *Causalité, permamence et réalité phenomenales*, Paris: Publications Universitaires de Louvan, Editions Beatrice-Nauwelaerts.

Montangero, J. (1984) 'Perspectives actuelles sur la psychogenèse du temps', *L'Année Psychologique, 84*, pp. 433–60.

Morison, P. and Gardner, H. (1978) 'Dragons and dinosaurs: the child's capacity to differentiate fantasy from reality'. In *Child Development, 49*(3), pp. 642–8.

Nicolas of Cusan (1979) *Works*, in two volumes. Vol. 1, Moscow: Mysl Publ.

Piaget, J. (1926) *La Representation du monde chez l'enfant*, Paris: Alcan.

Piaget, J. (1927) *La Causalité physique chez l'enfant*, Paris: Alcan.

Piaget, J. (1936) *La Naissance de l'intelligence chez l'enfant*, Neuchâtel–Paris: Delachaux et Niestlé.

Piaget, J. (1937a) *La Construction du réel chez l'enfant*, Neuchâtel–Paris: Delachaux et Niestlé.

Piaget, J. (1937b) *La Formation du symbole chez l'enfant*, Neuchâtel–Paris: Delachaux et Niestlé.

Piaget, J. (1946a) *Les Notions de mouvement et de vitesse chez l'enfant*, Paris: Press Universitaires de France.

Piaget, J. (1946b) *Le Developpement de la notion de temps chez l'enfant*, Paris: Presses Universitaires de France.

Piaget, J. (1967) *La Psychologie de l'intelligence*, Paris: Colin.

Piaget, J. and Inhelder, B. (1951) *La Genèse de l'idée de hasard chez l'enfant*, Paris: Presses Universitaires de France.

Piaget, J. and Inhelder, B. (1963) *The Child's Conception of Space*, London: Routledge & Kegan Paul.

Piaget, J., Inhelder, B. and Szeminska, A. (1948) *La Géométrie spontanée de l'enfant*, Paris: Presses Universitaires de France.

Piaget, J. and Szeminska, A. (1950) *La Genèse du nombre chez l'enfant*, Paris–Neuchâtel: Delachaux et Niestlé.

Plato (1952) *The Works*. In *Great Books of the Western World*, 7: *Plato*, Chicago–Toronto–Geneva: Encyclopaedia Britannica.

Plato (1968) *Works*, in three volumes. Vol. 1, Moscow: Mysl publ.

Plato (1972) *Works*, in three volumes. Vol. 3, Part 2, Moscow: Mysl Publ.

Powers, M. K. and Dobson, V. (1982) 'Effect of focus on visual acuity of human infants'. In *Vision Research, 22*(5), pp. 521–8.

Prawat, R. S., Anderson, A. H. and Hapkiewicz, W. (1983) 'Is the scariest monster also the least real? An examination of children's reality classifications'. In *The Journal of Genetic Psychology, 146*(2), pp. 7–12.

Prazdny, S. (1980) 'A computational study of a period of infant object-concept development', *Perception, 9*(2), pp. 125–50.

Prigogine, I. and Stengers, I. (1986) *Order from Chaos. New Dialogue of Man and Nature*, Moscow: Progress Publ.

Ramsay, D. S. and Campos, J. J. (1975) 'Memory by the infant in an object notion task'. In *Developmental Psychology, 11*(3), pp. 411–12.

Ramsay, D. S. and Campos, J. J. (1978). 'The onset of representation and entry into stage 6 of object permanence development'. In *Developmental Psychology, 14*(2), pp. 79–86.

Raspe, C. (1924) 'Kindliche Selbstbeobachtung und Theorienbildung'. In *Zeitschrift für angewandte Psychologie, 23*, pp. 302–28.

Russell, J. and Mitchell, P. (1985) 'Things are not always as they seem: the appearance–reality distinction and conservation'. In *Educational Psychology, 5*(3–4), pp. 227–38.

Schuberth, R. E., Werner, J. S. and Lipsitt, L. P. (1978) 'The stage IV error in Piaget's theory of object concept development: a reconsideration of the spatial localisation hypothesis'. In *Child Development, 49*(3), pp. 744–8.

Schultz, T. R., Fisher, G. W., Pratt, C. C. and Rulf, S. (1986) 'Selection of causal rules'. In *Child Development, 57*, pp. 143–52.

Schwartz, R. G. (1980) 'Presuppositions and children's metalinguistic judgements: concepts of life and the awareness of animacy restrictions'. In *Child Development, 51*(2), pp. 364–71.

Sextus Empiricus (1976) *Works, Book 1*, Moscow: Mysl Publ.

Slater, A., Morison, V. and Rose, D. (1982) 'Visual memory at birth'. In *British Journal of Psychology, 73*, pp. 519–25.

Smullyan, R. M. and Raymond, M. (1982) *The Lady or the Tiger?: and Other Logic Puzzles*, New York: Alfred Knopf.

Soroka, S. M., Corter, C. M. and Abramovitch, R. (1979) 'Infant's tactual discrimination of novel and familiar tactual stimuli'. In *Child Development, 50*(4), pp. 1251–3.

Staley, A. A. and O'Donnell, J. P. (1984) 'A developmental analysis of mothers' reports of normal children's fears'. In *The Journal of Genetic Psychology, 144*, pp. 165–78.

Starkey, P., Spelke, E. S. and Gelman, R. (1983) 'Detection of intermodal numerical correspondences by human infants'. In *Science, 222*, pp. 179–81.

Stern, W. (1923) *Psychologie der frühen Kindheit bis zum sechsten Lebensjahre*, Leipzig: Quell & Meyer.

Stolin, V. V. (1976) *Issledovanija porozhdenija zritelnogo prostranstvennogo obzasa* (Investigations of the genesis of a visual spatial image). In *Perception and Activity*, Moscow: Moscow Univ. Publ. pp. 101–208.

Stratton, G. (1896) 'Some preliminary experiments on vision without inversion of the retinal image'. In *Psychological Review, 3*, pp. 611–17.

Subbotsky, E. V. (1978) 'O pristrastuosti detskogo suzhdenija' (Bias in children's judgements), *Voprosy Psikhologii, 2*, pp. 81–90.

Subbotsky, E. V. (1983) *Problemy genezisa litchnosti* (Problems of the Genesis of Personality), Moscow: VINTI publ.

Subbotsky, E. V. (1985) 'Preschool children's perception of unusual phenomena'. In *Soviet Psychology*, Vol. 23, No. 3, pp. 91–114.

Subbotsky, E. V. (1986) 'A child's conception of the relationship between bodily and mental phenomena'. In *Soviet Psychology, 25*, pp. 61–90.

Subbotsky, E. V. (1990a) 'The preschooler's conception of the permanence of an object (Verbal and Actual Behavior), *Soviet Psychology, 28*, 3, pp. 42–67.

Subbotsky, E. V. (1990b) 'Phenomenal and rational perception of some object relations by preschoolers', *Soviet Psychology, 28*, 5, pp. 5–24.

Subbotsky, E. V. (1991a) 'A life span approach to object permanence', *Human Development, 34*, pp. 125–37.

Subbotsky, E. V. (1991b) 'Existence as a psychological problem: Object permanence in adults and preschool children', *International Journal of Behavioral Development, 14*, 1, pp. 67–82.

Subbotsky, E. V. (1992a) 'Early rationality and magical thinking in preschoolers: Space and time', *British Journal of Developmental Psychology* (submitted).

Subbotsky, E. V. (1992) 'Cognitive behaviour in unexplainable situations: Object permanence in adults' (submitted).

Subbotsky, E. and Trommsdorff, G. (1991) 'Object permanence in adults: a cross-cultural perspective', *Psychologische Beiträge*.

Tailor, M. and Flavell, J. H. (1984) 'Seeing and believing: children's understanding of the distinction between appearance and reality', *Child Development, 55*, pp. 1710–20.

Tomasello, M., Farrar, M. J. (1984) 'Cognitive bases of lexical development: Object permanence and relational words', *Journal of Child Language, 11*(3), pp. 477–93.

Tomasello, M., Farrar, M. J. (1986). 'Object permanence and relational words: A lexical training study', *Journal of Child Language, 13*(3), pp. 495–505.

Tul'viste, P. (1991) *A Cultural-Historical Approach to the Development of Verbal Thinking*, New York: Nova Press.

Tul'viste, P. (1982) 'Is there a form of verbal thought specific to childhood?' *Soviet Psychology, 21*, pp. 3–17.

Vandenberg, B. (1983–4) 'Play, logic and reality', *Imagination, Cognition and Personality, 3*(4), pp. 353–63.

Vandenberg, B. (1985) *Play, Myth and Hope*. Invited presentation to PAOS International Conference on Play, Amsterdam, September.

Venger, A. A. (1958) 'Rasvitie ponimanija pzichinnosti u detej doshkolnogo vozrasta' (The development of the understanding of causality in preschool-age children), *Voprosy psichologii*, 2.

Vygotsky, L. S. (1982) 'Myshlenije i retch' (Thought and Language). In L. S. Vygotsky, *Works*, in six volumes, Vol. 2, Moscow: Pedagogica Publ.

Wachs, T. D. (1975). 'Relation of infants' performance on Piaget scales between 12 and 24 months and their Stanfard-Binet performance at 31 months'. In *Child Development, 46*, pp. 929–35.

Wagner, S., Winner, E., Cicchetti, D. and Gardner, H. (1981) ' "Metaphorical" mapping in human infants'. In *Child Development, 52*,(2), pp. 728–31.

Walker, A. S., Owsley, C. J., Megaw-Nyce, J., Gibson, E. J., Bahrick, L. (1980) 'Detection of elasticity as an invariant property of objects by young infants'. In *Perception, 9*(6), pp. 713–18.

Warren, W. H. (1977) 'Visual information for object identity in apparent movement'. In *Perception & Psychophysics, 21*(3), pp. 264–8.

Webb, R. A., Massar, B. and Nadolny, T. (1972) 'Information and strategy in the young child's search for hidden objects', *Child Development, 43*(1), pp. 91–104.

Wellman, H. M. and Estes, D. (1986) 'Early understanding of mental entities: a re-examination of childhood realism'. In *Child Development, 57*(4), pp. 910–23.

Werner, H. (1948) *The Comparative Psychology of Mental Development*, New York: International Universities Press.

Wertsch, J. (1991). *Voices of the Mind: A sociocultural approach to mediated action*, Cambridge, Mass.: Harvard University Press.

Williamson, P. A., Kelley, M. F. and Waters, B. (1982) 'Animistic thought in young children: effects of probing'. In *Perceptual and Motor Skills, 54*, pp. 463–6.

Zaporozhetz, A. V. and Lukov, F. L. (1941) 'Pro rozvitok mirkuvannija u ditiny molodshego viku' (On the development of thinking in a young child), *Scientific Reports of the Charckov Pedagogical Institute*, vol. 5.

Zusne, L. (1985) 'Magical thinking and parapsychology'. In P. Kurtz (ed.), *A Skeptic's Handbook of Parapsychology*, New York: Prometheus Books, pp. 688–700.

Zusne, L. and Jones, W. H. (1982) *Anomalistic Psychology. A study of extraordinary phenomena of behavior and experience*. Hillsdale, N.J.: Erlbaum.

Subject Index

Name Index

Alexander, K. R., 115
Anaxogorus, 141
Aristotle, 13, 26, 141, 142
Arnheim, R., 28
Arseniev, A. S., 16, 17

Bacon, F., 27, 142
Baillargeon, R., 43, 117
Ball, W., 83
Beveridge, M., 83
Bower, T. G. R., 43, 116
Brain, M. D. S., 35
Bremner, J. G., 115
Bühler, K., 1, 3
Bullok, M., 83
Butterworth, G., 43

Campos, J. J., 43, 44, 52
Carey, S., 83
Cole, M., 128
Cossette-Ricard, M., 43

Davies, M., 83
Dembo, T., 107
Democritus, 7, 17, 112
Descartes, R., 3, 7, 13, 76, 142, 143
Diodor Kron, 112
Dobson, W., 115
Durkheim, E., 79, 127

El'konin, D. B., 28

Epicurus, 17, 112
Escher, M., 25, 31
Estes, D., 33
Evans-Pritchard, E. E., 127

Farrar, M. J., 42
Flavell, J. H., 35–7, 103
Frazer, J., 79, 127
Freeman, N. H., 43
Freud, S., 1, 3, 15, 16, 26, 32, 128

Gardner, H., 32
Gelman, R., 83
Gibson, E. J., 22, 115, 116
Gibson, J. J., 22, 112, 116
Gilat, I., 117
Girnis, S. V., 105
Golinkoff, R. M., 83
Goods, N. S., 117
Gottfried, A. W., 116
Gouin Décarie, T., 43
Gratch, G., 43, 51, 52
Gregory, R. L., 20, 25
Grivtsov, A. P., 107

Hagleitner, L., 83
Haith, M. M., 43
Hamer, R. D., 115
Harris, P. L., 34, 43, 44, 117
Hegel, G., 143

Name Index